# The Outspokin' Cyclist

## Phillip Barron

Avenida Books || 2011
Minneapolis, Minnesota

The outspokin' cyclist / Phillip Barron
Published by Avenida Books

ISBN 978-0-9827530-1-9 (paperback edition)

1. Cycling – Social aspects 2. Culture 3. Bicycle columnist I. Title
Sports & Recreation : Cycling
Sports & Recreation : Essays

Avenida Books

A |V

Minneapolis, Minnesota

*To Nancy*

# Contents

## Section I: Why Ride?                                                1

## Section II: Building a Bike Community                              21

# Section III: A World of Cycling    87

"Respetame, soy un ciclista" | "Respect me, I am a cyclist," graffiti (Quito, Ecuador)

# Preface

I am a cyclist.

To say as much sounds strange to me. Not because it isn't true, but because it is true. Riding a bicycle – for transportation, for errands, for joy – is something I do without thinking a whole lot about it. Pedaling is such a part of my identity that to call it out in the utterance "I am a cyclist" is to call attention to the idea that it could be otherwise. To say "I am a cyclist" when I choose to pedal a bicycle to work, to the grocery store, and along trails in the woods is akin to saying "I am a breather" or "I am someone who eats." Both are true, but both are also trivially true. For either to be otherwise would convey that I am no longer alive. And once, I came close to knowing what it would be like not to be a cyclist.

In March 2008, I had a mountain bike accident that left me nearly unable to ride a bicycle. It was a painful fall, one in which I broke teeth, hyper-extended tendons in my neck, and nearly paralyzed myself. But, like many accidents, its full effects were not known for several days. With the impression that my helmet took the brunt of the impact and that I had navigated my fall relatively unscathed, I finished pedaling the trail I had set out to ride, albeit more cautiously. Only through x-rays and subsequent conversations with doctors did I realize the extent of the damage I had done.

While I did not break any bones, I did break something else: a lifetime of trust in my body.

I now understand that I have two degrees of inner-ear balance, on and off. Since I was a child, I have prided myself on an above average ability to balance. I learned to ride a bike quickly. When it was time in gym class to perform fitness tests, I could stand on one foot longer than anyone else. When stretching my quads before a swim race, I would stand immovably on one foot while I pulled the other upwards to the backside of my skimpy Speedo racing suit. I even attribute the ease with which I learned to juggle to my instinct not to lean forward while tossing the bean bags up in the air, as most new jugglers do.

Having impeccable balance has obvious benefits while cycling.

I can track stand – stand on the pedals while the bike makes no forward or rearward motion – through stoplight changes with ease. Riding on the road, in a group, I have no trouble drafting others or "keeping a line" with companions. When climbing a steep stretch of singletrack, especially on long and rocky climbs, my ability to balance at slow speeds is the difference between pedaling to the summit and hike-a-bike. And riding skinnies, oh how I love to ride skinnies.

A skinny is a piece of wood steadied between two raised elements. The wood needs to be strong enough to carry the weight of a rider, and the supports need to be solid enough not to move while the rider climbs onto and off of the narrow strip. Skinnies might serve a real purpose, such as bridging two banks of a creek. But just as often, they are artificial (and fun) obstacles in the middle of a mountain bike trail. They might be rough hewn or smooth as a sidewalk. They might be constructed from cedar logs or garage-built from pressure treated lumber. Whatever form they take, skinnies are a challenge to riders because of the speed with which you approach them (especially when you do not know they are just around the bend), the psychological discomfort of having to stick to such a tight line (occasionally with real risks), and the focus required to climb, ride, dismount, and most importantly, to do it all so smoothly that it looks natural.

The morning after the opening night of an art show that I had curated, a show gathering historic photographs of bicycles in Durham, North Carolina, I took an out-of-town friend for a ride at a local mountain bike trail. It is a trail I have ridden countless times and have seen evolve over the years from a well-kept secret to a popular week-end destination. While I was demonstrating how to ride a skinny, my inner-ear decided to stop sending balance information to the rest of my body. It was a version of vertigo.

Growing up, I thought that "vertigo" was a condition where I might see the world move or even spin in front of my eyes. Instead, the onset of vertigo is not something I see. It is something I feel. Rather than seeing the world spin in front of me, everything looks normal. On that March day, the vertiginous signals that knocked me off balance came from my inner-ear. My cochlea, the conch shell shaped bone in the inner-ear, swelled with endolymphatic fluid and could not deter-mine whether I was standing upright, lying on my side, standing on my head, or twirling – or so my doctors tell me later. In other words, my trusted sense of balance abandoned me, choosing a precarious moment to do so. I fell from the skinny, but because my sense of bal-ance was not working properly, I did not feel the fall; I only saw it. The only signal I received that I was falling was visual. I felt the impact, however. Landing upside down, crushing my helmet, I instinctively rolled forward in a motion that saved me from snapping my neck.

Reflecting on the accident in the days that followed, I lost faith in that most basic relationship: the one between my mind and my body. That my mind knows how to talk to my body, to tell my legs to move or arms to throw, is a mystery – I cannot explain how it happens – but it is one that I accept and have accepted all of my life. Vertigo, however, had the effect of pulling apart this symbiosis, causing me (if I am my mind) to doubt my body. Vertigo caused my accident; fear that vertigo would return at any moment kept me off my bicycle for the next two years.

Learning not to trust your body is not just devastating. It is alienating. Your whole experience in life is interpreted through the body, so when your body fails you in an important way, the shock of it invites withdrawal and introspection. I do not know whether the 17th century French philosopher René Descartes played any sports, but athletes are by nature of what they do well-suited to understand Cartesian problems. Descartes's mind-body problem is a thought experiment, the stock and trade technique used by philosophers. It goes like this.

There are two kinds of phenomena in this world: mental and physical. Everything you know about the world outside of your mind (the physical world) is filtered through your senses. You know what an orange looks like when you see it. You know the texture of its subtle undulate surface and round shape when you feel it. You know its bright, sharp taste when you chew it and those packets of citrus juice squirt onto your tongue. You know its aroma when you break the zest, peel back pieces of the thick rind, and smell it. And to the extent that oranges make any noise, perhaps the thud one makes when it ripens and falls from the tree, you know its sound when you hear it. Nearly everything we know about the world, we know because of our senses.

Yet, having knowledge is a mental phenomenon. Mental activities – such as desiring, understanding, deciding, calculating, loving, and indeed knowing – take place in the mind and need not be precipitated by physical activities.

And therein lies a problem. How exactly physical phenomena

relate to mental phenomena is a question that perplexes philosophers, biologists, and cognitive scientists to this day. We know that they do relate. Seeing a frosted glass of fine crafted beer can remind me that I am thirsty. It might even amplify my desire to taste the bitter hops. But how does it do this?

We know too that our senses are prone to deception. I might think I see something that is not there. If I happen to be in the desert when I am thirsty, I might mistake the shimmering heat of the sand for a cool, irrigated oasis — or so goes the classic mirage story from the Bugs Bunny cartoons of my childhood. Perhaps the simplest example of sensory deception is that, when we dream, we believe that the events we experience in the dream are actually happening. While we are in the dream, we see sights, taste tastes, and feel feelings that we learn later are not actually sights, tastes, or feelings at all. They are sensations manufactured by our minds, so real that we believe them.

So, if our senses can fool us and our minds can build entire realities in which we falsely believe, then how do we know what it is that is actually happening? Ultimately, how do we know that that which we believe to be actual life is not just a dream from which we have yet to wake up? Such a clean, distinct separation between mind and body is all well and good in the comfort of the philosopher's armchair, but our everyday experience is more conceptual muddle. In the words of the erudite cyclist John Stilgoe, "a person is more than separated mind and body; the body exists as much to carry the mind as the mind exists to direct the body" (186). Athletes are in a position to grasp the mind-body problem intuitively since skilled athletes are keenly aware of the relationship between their mind and body. They have trained their bodies, directed by their minds, to do something very well. Most sports are premised on physical activity that does not come naturally. Riding a bike, for example, is a skill that you must learn. And once you can competently pilot a banana-seat cruiser along a flat stretch of asphalt, you can build your skill by riding a bike in less amenable environments: on grass, in sand, into a head wind, uphill, over roots, through creek beds, and even hucking off cliffs. With each new challenge and rising degree of difficulty, the more important it is for your senses - your body - to give your mind reliable information. I was already a mountain biker with philosophical learning; vertigo gave me new reasons to ponder the dangers, epistemological and otherwise, of trusting my senses.

It has taken two years of meditation on my particular version of the mind-body problem, dietary experimentation, and a three-thousand mile move to the bicycle capital of the United States for me to feel comfortable once again climbing aboard two wheels and testing whether I have successfully retrained myself to listen to visual inputs and ignore inner-ear inputs. So far, so good.

My two years off the bike were filled with the kind of existential angst that comes from being afraid to be yourself. During my retreat from the bicycle, I still thought of myself as a cyclist. In fact, it was probably during that time that I recognized myself most clearly as one. I missed riding, and it was difficult to realize that I wanted to ride and was afraid to.

I am happy once again to be "that guy who always bikes to work." "Even in the rain?" "Even in the rain." I am happy once again to be that guy who the grocery store clerks ask (when they see my helmet and count the bags), "do you need any help getting this home today?" I am happy once again to be the object of a neighborhood kid's noticing, "there goes that guy with the long bike."

Of course, in Davis, California, which has a reputation for having more bikes than cars, more bike racks than parking spaces, and more cyclists per capita than anywhere else I have lived, I am also happy to be riding along without much attention paid to the fact that I am a cyclist.

Notes:

Stilgoe, John. *Outside Lies Magic.* Walker & Company. 1998. Print.

# The Outspokin' Cyclist

From 2004 through 2008, it was forward thinking of *The Herald Sun* to reserve space in its pages for a bicycle columnist. I cannot comment objectively on the wisdom of hiring me to fill that space, but on a regular basis the newspaper set aside room in its printed conversation for alternative ways of thinking about transportation. Not many newspapers do this. In the time that I wrote columns for Durham readers, I can only hope that Bull City subscribers enjoyed reading the columns as much as I enjoyed the researching, the interviewing, and the writing that went into them. *The Herald Sun* published more than sixty of my columns in all.

Writing a regular column is a bit of a balancing act, swaying back and forth between timeliness and timelessness. When reflecting on which pieces were appropriate for compiling and republishing in this book, my editor and I removed columns that we felt were too much indebted to a moment in time. Of the columns which we selected to appear here, I chose not to update them, since updating would have led to rewriting, and more often than not rewriting would have removed the connection to the inspiration behind the column. I offer this bound version of my columns as a collective example of what a newspaper and a city can do to support its cycling community.

In the summer of 2008, I attended the Los Angeles installation of the Bicycle Film Festival. The international event captures in its film submissions the breadth of appeal, utility, and beauty of the humble bicycle. I was struck most by the diversity of experiences set to rhythm and made glamorous on screen, worthy of the Hollywood venue for the films' projection.

From the daredevils who bomb mountain slopes and skitch taxi-cabs to the pirouettes of flatland BMXers and the Seattle fixie scene; from the post-punk urban cycling scene and post-apocalyptic vision of Chunk 666 to the aimless sand drawings of a man, his bike, and his rake; from Craig MacLean's uber-planned training program for track cycling's world cup to Matthew Modine's Bicycle for a Day, the films all shared one thing: two wheels.

Likewise, I am a pluralist when it comes to the cycling community. I believe that we need space in our cities and mountains for people of all kinds to ride bicycles for all kinds of reasons. In "The Outspokin' Cyclist," I documented multiple cycling communities in Durham: the mountain bikers and the lycra-clad roadies, the fixed-gear alleycat races and the fundraising rides, the kids experimenting with two-wheeled freedom on a bike path and the septuagenarian Durhamite training to ride across Israel for better relations between Israel and Palestine. They all have a home in Durham, and for four years, they all had a place in the hometown newspaper.

Caution: bicycling can be addictive (Durham, NC)

# Acknowledgements

Neither the book before you nor the columns I wrote for Durham, North Carolina's daily newspaper, *The Herald Sun*, would have been possible without the help of many people. While I cannot thank individually the hundreds of people who agreed to be interviewed for columns, I would be remiss not to thank just a few folks who made exceptional contributions: Bob Ashley, Ron Landfried, and Nancy Wykle for seeing the important role that *The Herald Sun* could play in giving Durham's bicycling community a regular voice; Mark Schultz and Anne Krishnan deserve both thanks and credit for giving a novice a chance to develop into a columnist; Diane Daniel for her insight into column writing; members of the Bicycle and Pedestrian Advisory Committee for encouragement; and finally all of *The Herald Sun*'s readers who voiced support and criticism through the Letters to the Editor section of the newspaper.

For help locating the historic photos in "Women's Liberation Through Cycling," thanks to Elizabeth Dunn, Research Services Librarian at Duke University, Lynn Richardson, librarian of the North Carolina Collection at the Durham County Library, Gary Kueber, and Milo Pyne.

Thanks to my brother Andrew for encouraging me to revisit these columns just as I am returning to the bicycle itself. My parents, Brian and Debbie, deserve special recognition for teaching me to ride a bike, for upgrading the bicycles of my childhood as soon as I would break them, for their patience with me in emergency rooms when I broke parts of myself, for picking me up on the other side of town when I had ridden too far, and most of all for the freedom to explore the world from two wheels. Thanks to my brother Matt for exploring mountain biking with me in the early, pre-suspension days. Our shoulders will never be the same.

Thanks to Matt, Brianna, and Alicia, to Ursula and Lauren, and to Summer and Darius for keeping me young, despite all the gray hair.

And to my friend, Nancy Gallman, thank you for always reminding me that anything worth saying is honest.

# Section I: Why Ride?

To climb onto a bicycle and become the engine is a fundamentally transforming experience – a creative experience.

Richard Florida, *Rise of the Creative Class*

Members of the TORC chapter of the Mountain Bike Patrol on a training ride on the Beaver Dam trails (Wake County, NC)

# Bicycling can become way of life

I ride a bicycle for many reasons.

It is healthy – riding my bike for an hour to and from work every day is a reasonable workout. It's fun – there's nothing like mountain biking in Pisgah National Forest. It costs less than driving a car – I save a lot of money on gas. It's a cleaner mode of transportation than any automobile – the Triangle region has some of the worst air quality in the nation. Converting food to energy is a lot cleaner and more efficient than converting gasoline to energy.

Phillip Barron

But most of all, I ride because of how it makes me feel.

On two wheels, I feel more connected to the neighborhoods I ride through. People are friendlier to me when I'm on a bike. You see more from the saddle of a bicycle than you do from behind the windows of a car or bus. Every morning when I wake up, I look forward to the coolness of the "kudzu corridor" (also known as the American Tobacco Trail, Durham's longest Rail-to-Trail bike path). No matter how hectic things get at work, I know that my mind will quiet once my pedals find a rhythm.

In this column, I want to do several things. If you already enjoy spending time on two wheels, then I want to share with you my love of the bicycle. I'll tell you about some of Durham's bicycling events and keep you informed about what the City Council and County Commissioners are doing to help make bicycling a viable alternative mode of transportation.

If you don't ride much, but you want to ride more, then I want to help make bicycling more accessible to you. I plan to spend some time talking about how to perform simple repairs to your bike, how to commute to work, how to ride in the rain or ride at night. I'll also try to highlight some of the best places to ride as well as some ways to fit bicycling into your busy schedule. Durham has a growing bicycling community and I'll help you get in touch with it.

If you're not a bicyclist at all, then maybe you'll enjoy some of my stories and live a bicyclist's life vicariously.

I also want to hear from you. I hope you'll e-mail me with questions, comments on the column or just to share good news.

So, ride around and say hello to the folks you pass. If you don't already know how much fun bicycling is, you'll find out soon enough.

*This column appeared in The Herald Sun in July 2004.*

Eno Quarry (Durham, NC)

# Take time to unplug, be outside and watch the sunset

There was a year when I watched the sunset almost every evening. Across the street from the school I was attending at the time began a neighborhood of houses that had been built in the 1950s. These streets and dwellings brought unprecedented order to the post-war town, carving their grid-like stamp into Southern countryside. The streets parallel to the main road separating the campus from the neighborhood ran only four or five deep, and the last street had houses on only one side. The far side of the street faced an open pasture where a farmer kept cattle.

The thin drainage ditch and barbed-wire fence formed an artificial boundary between the built environment and the natural, but it felt like the edge of the world each evening I sat there. Facing the trees on the far side of the pasture, you are facing due west.

I rode my bike to the same spot on that road each evening. After eating in the dining hall and before buckling down with books for the night, I rode through the twilit streets. I made no secret of this cyclical ritual, so occasionally friends rode with me. Tommy once tried to dance with the cows that were dining alongside the fence. Jennifer sat with me one evening before leaving for Honduras. Kimberly shared the sunset with me a few times years before she served and died in Iraq. Leighton, Joey, Josh, and Cathy each joined me other evenings. But mostly I sat there on the eastern side of the drainage culvert, bike on its side next to me, alone. And I sat there to make a daily point of being outdoors.

In the process of describing the physics of sunset, Christopher Dewdney, in his meditation on all things nocturnal *Acquainted with the Night*, tells of a group of friends, nature lovers, peace seekers, poets, and fellow scholars which gathers to watch the sunset each evening in Toronto. And although he explains both the science and mystery of that planetary spectacle, he talks too about the healthy reasons he looks west with friends each night.

Durham is a green city. It is flush with trees, both deciduous and evergreen alike. Trees that astound you with color, like the fall fashion show on Wrightwood Avenue, or with grandeur, like the amazing hundreds of years old oak on old Erwin Road between Dry Creek Road and Mt. Moriah. Even as we lose acres of forest each year to development, Durham is still a lush environment. All of which mean that Durham is a great city in which to be outdoors.

Bike commuters know that an outdoors activity after work brings a different perspective to daily life. So do the folks who walk the tracks at Shepard Middle School and Durham School of the Arts, as well as members of Duke's employees' Live for Life running and walking clubs who walk and run the gravel path around Duke's east campus each week. The city's open spaces and trails, from Whip-poorwill Park to the New Hope Bottomlands Trail, are designed just for a morning or evening stroll, ride, or skate.

As we come out of the sickly-saturated consumerism of the holiday season, the empty promises of the cell phone and the plasma TV may catch up with you – especially around the time the first credit card bill comes in. These empty promises have to do with buying into the ideas that we need to surround ourselves with electronic stimuli and that everything we need is indoors. But the iPod generation needs to know there is a life without electronic media.

A recent Scientific American reported that women who worked out regularly had about half the risk of colds as those who did not exercise. Public health officials agree that being outside in sunlight for 45 minutes a day contributes to your health. It strengthens your immune system and is the most efficient way for your body to generate the Vitamin D needed for health.

But absorbing healthy Vitamin D is not the only reason to step

Phillip Barron

out of doors. Since most people spend most of their time indoors, the experience of outdoor environments is a refreshing transition. It does as much for your mental health as exercise does for your body.

How would our lives be different if we each found time each day to unplug and adopt a low-tech outdoors habit like walking around the neighborhood? Why not take an evening bike ride with a friend?

As for me, I'm still looking for a place in Durham to watch the sunset.

*This column appeared in The Herald Sun in January 2007.*

# Make some idle time to relearn lost art of exploring

You see more from a bicycle than you do from a car. You see even more from a balloon-tire Schwinn than you do from a carbon fiber Pinarello.

That's why author John Stilgoe, in *Outside Lies Magic*, says to choose the cruiser.

"Bicycle to the store," he says, "then ride down the alley toward the railroad tracks, bump across the uneven bricks by the loading dock grown up in thistle and chicory, pedal harder uphill toward the

Victorian houses converted into funeral homes, make a quick circuit of the school yard, coast downhill…, tail the city bus for a mile or two, swoop through a multilevel parking garage, glide past the firehouse back door, slow down and catch your reflection in the plate-glass windows."

Where's Stilgoe taking us? Nowhere in particular; and that's the point of exploring.

You know, if only intuitively, what he's talking about. There's something nice about packing a lunch and riding off in no particular direction in search only of finding something new. It's not destination riding, it's not about exercise, it's about wandering. Exploring by bike is a way of reevaluating our everyday environment, the setting we're always in, and discovering mysterious and fascinating parts of our community we overlook.

With the right mindset, two lost arts can come together on a bicycle.

First is the lost art of appreciating something for its own sake. There's not a whole lot of unstructured time in our daily lives. I think there's not enough.

In response to the hurried lifestyle of 1920s Oxford, England, philosopher Bertrand Russell wrote an essay extolling the virtues of idleness. He reminds us that work, or moving stuff around, is not the point of life. If it were the point, then we might think that anything that doesn't help us make more money, improve our test scores, or get a nicer house is not worth doing.

Oh, wait. There are a lot of us who really believe that. If you're one of them, then you've fallen victim to what Russell calls "the cult of efficiency." Valuing only time spent productively can lead us to believe that our lifestyles dictate a maddening pace.

Don't worry, there's a way out. There's a way to reclaim some of that time, a way to set your own pace.

Some things are worth doing just for the sake of doing them. One of those things worth doing all by itself is exploring. The art of exploring is the second lost art.

Exploring is just looking closely at the things you pass every day and pausing to consider their meaning. Exploring is simple, and it's accessible to all of us.

Exploring, in this way, is not about being the first to climb a mountain or photograph a waterfall. Jill Homer, a cyclist and journalist in Juneau, Alaska, says "my opinion about exploration has always been that if I've never been there, it's new to me." And that's the kind of exploring we all can do.

Back in Durham, neighbor John Schelp says he likes to explore the American Tobacco Trail.

"The ATT is a wonderful place to see the seasons change," says Schelp. "The crisp fall air brings all sorts of new colors along the length of the trail, and it's neat to see the changes in the little gardens. These quiet urban spots remind me of my time in Congo and China, where vegetable gardens stretch to the edges of public paths or little foot bridges reach over ditches."

As Schelp hints, part of exploring is noticing what's there. The other part is making a connection with what you find.

The joy of exploring is in not knowing what you'll find. Have you ridden the alleyways of Durham's downtown neighborhoods? Do you know Durham's many murals? Most are painted on the sides of buildings downtown and along Fayetteville St. Have you found the Eno Quarry? To the few who know it, it's a nice swimming hole. Do you know where there's a good spot to watch the sunset? Do you know which marching band practices on the field behind CC Spaulding Elementary School?

There's no map that will point you toward these Durham treasures. But, they're examples of what you might find if you're out exploring. You're not likely to find them if you're in a car, because most of the time they lie beyond where cars can go.

If you try exploring for yourself, leave the heart rate monitor and spandex at home. Don't run any errands. Just ride. See where you end up. And if you find anything interesting, let me know.

*This column appeared in The Herald Sun in November 2006.*

# SSpots of Time

Sweet are those moments when all your skills converge and you clear a technical section with more grace than you thought possible. That's what I call flow. Others call it groovin' or dialed-in. "'Spots of time' was the phrase Wordsworth used for such moments," says writer Ron Rash, "but the poet's words were no better than mine because what I felt was beyond any words that had ever been used before. You need a new language." I hope you've experienced what I'm talking about. It's a rush like no other. In the mountain bike community, there are as many reasons to ride as there are riders. It took 15 years of mountain biking and the experience of single-speed mountain biking for me to realize explicitly what I'd known only implicitly all along: to me, finding flow is my reason to ride.

For William Wordsworth, "spots of time" were key moments in his life. They formed remarkably vivid memories. He talks about the compression of time, the heightened senses, the feeling of being inside something important. He experienced spots most consistently in nature, and although many call his experiences mystical Wordsworth denied any supernatural element to these moments. Rather, they are about as grounded in this earth as you can get.

I ride to find that state of flow in the woods. This doesn't mean that I ride slowly or on flat trails. There is a state of grace that a rider can achieve while riding over roots and rocks, through rollercoasters and bowls, over logs and logstacks, and all the while maintain speed. Flow is possible on a technical trail – it is just harder to find. But, the difficulty reaching it is what makes it so rewarding. It is about dabbing less, stepping out of the pedals as little as possible. It is about accepting what comes around the corner. It is about loving the challenge of the trail laid out before me.

In a state of flow I briefly forget that my bike and I are two separate things. I forget that I am a clumsy bi-ped who ca not move gracefully down a mountain without help. I forget that it should not be possible to travel this fast over roots, rocks, twists, and turns. I move so smoothly, so instinctively that it is difficult to say that I am responsible for my movements, since no deliberate act of will could fit so harmoniously into the environment. When in flow, I am not totally in control of my actions. There is something else going on, something more than me, a bike, and a path. It is as though the three merge temporarily. Flow never lasts long – usually no longer than a few seconds at a time. But these moments, scattered throughout a two hour ride, convey a lifetime of experience.

The lifetime, the wisdom of these moments is what interests me most. Nietzsche took moments like these as evidence that the there is no end-point at which history is aiming. He knew, because he experienced moments of clarity where all the wisdom of eternity seemed within reach, that the present contains within it everything we need to find meaning in the world. "The world is complete and reaches its finality at each and every moment. What could ten more years teach that the past ten were unable to teach!" I do not know history's aims or universal meanings, but I do know that the compression of time in these moments is something special. These moments are wise in the sense that every spot of time or moment of flow has taught me something. I have learned some new skill or that I am capable of something I had not experienced before. Compressed time is not the same as time slowed down. Time slows down when you fall. You know you have lost your balance, you know you are past that critical point where you could have caught yourself, you know you are going to slam your shoulder into that rock. It all happens in slow motion, maybe because your mind is working twice as fast as normal.

Compressed time is not slow – if anything, it is time sped up. Maybe this is where we recover the time that slows down when we fall. Nor are spots of time or sessions of flow inevitable. When you fall, the crunch of the shoulder to the rock is inevitable; every thought that races through your mind before the crunch just delays what is guaranteed. Falling, no matter how drawn out, has a clear end. You see it coming.

But a spot of time is different; experiencing one is not guaranteed. Nor is it clear, while you are in one, how long it will last or even whether it will end. When you are in a spot of time, you are not conscious of anything else – not even the fact that you are in it. You realize what just happened only when it is over.

More than irregular, spots of time are also elusive. I never experience one when I try to. I know I am more likely to experience one in the saddle of my single-speed than in front of a glowing computer monitor, but that is about it.

Before going single, I had my own ideas what to expect: tougher climbs; more cautious, thoughtful riding; struggling to keep momentum. What I was not prepared for was how quickly I felt freed from thinking about speeds and gears. My first few single-speed rides were experiences in liberation. I was focusing on the trail, not on the bike. I am very comfortable with my bike – I have had it for four years, I have 6,000+ off-road miles on it, and I have ridden it up and down the East Coast. But as a single-speed is the first time that the bike moves like it is an extension of me and not just a machine I manipulate. As a geared bike, at best, I just manipulated it well. Now, before turns or hills, I spend my time picking my lines, not my gears. Keeping momentum on climbs is a challenge of a different sort, though not as difficult as I expected.

Some people insist that a spot of time is something experienced in stillness. That clarity is something you achieve through meditation, cross-legged on the floor staring at a candle flame. Maybe. Like Wordsworth and Rash, I meditate in motion. There is a stillness, a calm, within flow, but it is more spiritual than physical. The urge to mountain bike comes from the soul. Riding in the woods is a spiritual experience, but not a religious or even a mystical one. Like Wordsworth, I have found greater solace in staying firmly planted on dirt.

Standing on dirt with me, Norman Maclean says of the elusive nature of these moments that "poets talk about 'spots of time,' but it is really [fly] fishermen who experience eternity compressed into a moment. No one can tell what a spot of time is until suddenly the whole world is a fish and the fish is gone."

*This story first appeared in Bike Reader in November 2004.*

Teaching mountain bike safety at the Triangle's first Fat Tire Festival (Raleigh, NC)

# Section II: Building a Bike Community

Most U.S. cities are not very bike-friendly. They're not very pedestrian-friendly either. They're car-friendly — or at least they try very hard to be. In most of these cities one could say that the machines have won.

David Byrne, *Bicycle Diaries*

Fresh paint on Cornwallis Road, heading into Research Triangle Park

# Bike-friendly community needs planning

B uilding a bicycling community takes cooperation. Cooperation between drivers and cyclists. Cooperation between municipal and state governments. And, when our community grows, cooperation between the public and private spheres of development.

Historically, the model that Durham used for bicycle transportation improvements focused on responding to residents' requests. Encouraged by cyclists and bike activists, in 2001 the Durham City Council and the Durham County Commissioners jointly established the Durham Bicycle and Pedestrian Advisory Committee. It's charged with promoting "the full integration of bicycling [sic] into community transportation policies and practices." That is, the city and county want BPAC to help identify ways to make Durham more bike-friendly.

This is a radical departure from the "squeaky wheel gets the grease" policy and it sets Durham apart from most other cities. BPAC's charter establishes a body dedicated to helping the city address bicyclists' needs before the bicyclists raise them themselves. BPAC is not a replacement for citizen input; it's a complement.

BPAC's goal is to do what it can to make sure that bicycles and bicyclists are considered whenever public facilities are built, whenever a road is widened, whenever new land is acquired. Why? Because it's more cost-effective to stripe bike lanes while widening roads, to build sidewalks on the bridge when building the bridge.

This is part of building a bike-friendly community. But, the city can do only so much. The private sphere picks up where the public sphere leaves off.

Bike lanes invite cyclists as long as there is a place, at their destination, for cyclists to park their bikes safely. Public roads with bike lanes encourage more people to ride when the private neighborhood streets connecting to these roads are also bike friendly.

So, I have a few requests for help building a stronger bike community in the Triangle. Consider them end of the year requests or New Year's wishes.

First, let's host more cycling events. The Halloween Hundred drew more than 180 cyclists to its inaugural event and Little River Park's grand opening drew an estimated 200 mountain bikers. Cyclists have a strong presence in Durham and it's evident that riders come out to support homegrown events. How about a downtown criterium?

Second, a request to private businesses. Please, make sure that if someone (an employee, customer, or client) wanted to bike to your business that he or she could. Cyclists need a safe and secure place to park their bikes. Covered bike parking is ideal. And hey, while we're at it, why not encourage customers to bike by offering a discount on purchase totals? Whole Foods gives a bring-your-own-bag credit to encourage that good practice. Why not encourage another?

Third, to all those developers out there, please think of bicycles in all new planning and construction. Bike lanes and greenways are more useful when they connect to neighborhood bike paths or parks with bike racks.

Bike-friendly resources are gifts, not just to bicyclists, but to the Triangle as a whole. Promoting clean, healthy, person-powered transportation is about building a stronger sense of care and concern for our community.

*This column appeared in The Herald Sun in December 2004.*

Grocery shopping by bike and riding home down 8th Street in Davis, CA, the oldest bike lane in the United States.

# An inconsistent road is no road at all

I magine driving along when without signage, without warning, and without anywhere else to go, your lane ends. You stop, baffled, climb out of your car and look around. About 50 yards ahead you see where the road continues. Between here and there is an unpaved, patchy mix of grass, gravel, mounds of unused asphalt, and murky puddles from last night's rain. Even if you wanted to drive through this gap in the road, you're not sure you should since the ground is also littered with rusty car parts left by the last person who tried to traverse the stretch.

A motorist would immediately report the gap in the road to the local public works department. Such a gap would fail every known traffic engineering standard. Really, it's a lawsuit waiting to be filed.

Cyclists, however, know this scenario all too well. One minute we're riding comfortably on the 3 ft. shoulder of a wide outer lane. The next minute, we have to make a split-second decision: we can stop, jump off a six-inch ledge into the sandy grass just off the road (which is also usually filled with broken glass and empty fast-food bags), or suddenly merge with the automobile traffic.

Riding a bike in traffic isn't necessarily dangerous. Merging with automobile traffic without warning, however, is pretty scary.

The inconsistency of the shoulder, the width of pavement just outside the line marking the limit of the lane, is just one of the reasons why state law says that cyclists should ride in the travel lane, as part of traffic. Under state law, a bicycle is considered a vehicle, just like any car, motorcycle, or truck. Not only do bicyclists have the right to ride in traffic, it's also the safest place on the road to ride. Sometimes, though, uncooperative or unaware motorists or even just a steady stream of automobile traffic can marginalize bikers, pushing us to the shoulder.

Relegated to the margins of the roads, we often ride in that inconsistent, crumbling, glass-strewn space that may end abruptly. When the shoulder extends a foot or more in width, a cyclist can be tricked into thinking that the shoulder is a safe place to ride.

Old Erwin Rd. and Ephesus Church Rd. are case studies in varying shoulder widths and bottle-necking narrow bridges. At times, a cyclist can ride down Erwin on a width of pavement wide enough to be a bike lane. At the bottom of a hill, the "lane" may end without warning.

Roads with inconsistent shoulders are dangerous in their deception. They appear to offer bicyclists space to ride. On your bicycle, that car-free zone just outside the outer lane entices you. Then, you're forced to think quickly about how best to avoid an accident. Neither merging nor stopping are ideal.

What would be ideal? What if civil engineers and transportation planners thought about bicycles with every road designed and built? What if bike lanes on urban streets and wide outer lanes on rural roads were the rule rather than the exception? Then the problem of the inconsistent shoulder would be a thing of the past.

We don't accept this kind of dangerous inconsistency for our automobiles. Why do we accept it for our bikes?

*This column appeared in The Herald Sun in April 2005.*

Long shadows a December morning on the American Tobacco Trail. (Durham, NC)

# Bike commuting on the rise

In April 2004, I took a road trip to the Grand Canyon. Just inside the Arizona state line, I stopped for gas. I'd always heard that gas is more expensive on the west coast, and here was proof. The price of "premium" gas began with a "2" – I cleverly took a picture of the sign so that my friends back home could have a good laugh at gas prices in excess of $2 per gallon.

Now, the joke's on us.

Gas prices are hovering around $3 per gallon, and that's reason enough for me (and my wallet) to think twice about driving my car to Raleigh to go mountain biking. An October 6th Washington Post commodities article reports that while "SUV sales plunged in September more than 50 percent, U.S. bicycle sales have outnumbered car sales." Sounds like mine is not the only wallet taking a hit.

On my route to work, I've met more first-time bicycle commuters in the last two months than in the last two years. Heck, probably more than I've met in the last 5 years. But at most, my experience merely anecdotally suggests that ridership numbers may be up.

Is the national bicycle-sales trend holding true for Durham as well?

"We've definitely seen an increase in sales this year" says REI-Durham's store manager Jim Bennett. "And we certainly have seen a bigger increase in the last three months. The [Durham] store showed a 39% increase for the year through June, and since June we're up 59% over last year's sales."

Durham's other full service bicycle retailer, The Bicycle Chain has evidence to support the same trend. Chris Hull, the new general manager of the The Bicycle Chain's Durham store, says the store has definitely seen one of its best fall seasons in a long time. "Sales are up, business is up," he said.

But just as the New York Times bestseller list for books tells you nothing about whether people actually read the books they buy, new bicycle sales don't necessarily indicate new ridership.

An increase in business for bicycle repair shops, however, would suggest that people are riding the bikes they have.

"When people ride their bikes, they need to be repaired," says REI's Bennett. "Revenue we've taken in from the bike shop shows that people are riding their bikes as well."

Hull says The Bicycle Chain has also seen a significant increase in business for the service department. "People are dusting off their old bikes that have been sitting in the garage and bringing them in to get them in shape to ride," he said.

Whereas service customers are famous for making requests along the lines of, "just do the minimum to get the bike running again," Bennett says that customers are now taking bike maintenance more seriously.

"When people are willing to spend more money on their bikes, it's often because they are riding more regularly," Bennett says. "They're riding to work or school and need their bikes to be reliable."

Separating the effect of gas prices on bike sales from the effect of Lance Armstrong winning a 7th Tour de France may be difficult.

But Bennett says that REI has also seen an increase in the sale of commuter-specific accessories like fenders and racks. Although manufacturers are producing newer bike models with frame geometries designed specifically for commuting, you can also retro-fit just about any bike with the components that turn your sleek road bike or heavy duty mountain bike into a more utilitarian commuter – semi-slick tires for mountain bikes, locks, racks, panniers (saddlebags that hang over the racks), baskets, lights, and even reflective vests.

Components like fenders and tires with low rolling resistance make your everyday ride more comfortable. Cargo racks, panniers, and baskets make your bike more useful.

So, whether or not there are more folks riding to work due to higher prices at the gas pumps, there are more folks investing in bicycles and in the kind of equipment you'd use to ride to work.

Are there more new riders in Durham? I don't know. You tell me. And come tell me at the next Bicyclist Breakfast.

*This column appeared in The Herald Sun in October 2005.*

# In their own words... new bike commuters speak out

I asked new bicycle commuters in the Triangle area whether they had any thoughts to share on their decision to ride. Boy, did they.

This week, I'm letting some folks who started bicycle commuting within the last year step up to the microphone. Morning motorists, city council, and even you, sitting on fence about whether you can rely on your bike to get you to work — take note; these folks are talking to you.

Mostly for the exercise, Joseph Maxwell started bike commuting about seven months ago. Three days a week, he rides from Durham to Sports Endeavors (SEI) in Hillsborough.

"I am one of two bike commuters in a company of about 450 employees. There are many physically active employees at SEI, but I assume most people don't feel confident or safe riding into Hillsborough. But he says Highway 751 and Old NC 10 make for a a nice ride. A wider shoulder or bike lane on 751 (going out towards Highway 70) would be a great improvement. I see a lot of cyclists using this road. Obviously, bike lanes along my route to Hillsborough would make my commute easier. More than anything, I would just like for drivers to show more consideration towards cyclists."

Rhonda Kaye, a teacher at Lowe's Grove Middle School, started bike commuting when the new school year began in August.

Before then, she says, "I would drive to work by myself. I started riding for two main reasons: first, the cost of gas started to creep up and I thought riding would help my family save money. Then, after Hurricane Katrina, there was talk of a gas shortage, and I thought I would be a good citizen, and set an example for my students. So I started doing it 2-3 times a week."

"Cycling on a teacher's schedule can be a challenge. My work days starts at 7:15, so I don't have a big cushion of time to get to work and be ready to teach," says Kaye. "The one thing [sic] the city can do to make my ride easier is to add bike lanes on Sedwick Rd and Alston

Ave."

Dave Sokal would also like to see bike lanes or extra lane width on Sedwick and Alston. Sokal lives in Parkwood and bikes to work in Research Triangle Park, but he does not consider busy, narrow two-lane roads with no shoulders to be acceptable for safe commuting. His route to work is currently a mix of on-road riding with a shortcut on an unofficial trail he uses to avoid narrow, high volume roads.

Since she started riding in July, Kim Gray says that her biggest challenge has been negotiating with cars. "I think that the city could do more to educate its drivers through some sort of campaign." Gray says that she was able to get cyclists' rights pamphlets from Alison Carpenter, the City of Durham's Bicycle and Pedestrian transportation planner, and get her employer to distribute them through monthly paychecks. "If more places did that I think that would help," says Gray.

Tanya Jisa echoes Gray's wish for more public education about cyclists' rights. "There are lots of people who still don't 'get it' that bikes have just as much right and reason to be on the road as cars," she says.

Determined to commute by bike once she moved to Durham, Jisa sold her car before she ever left Decatur, Georgia. "Luckily I found a job with Duke just over 5 miles from my new home, so I made a few trial runs before my job officially began," she says.

"I started riding for fitness and health benefits – working my exercise time into my commute to and from work is a big bonus. I also like the opportunities to transition to and from work on a bike. Rather than getting in a car and 'fighting traffic', I get to have an enjoyable bike ride at my own pace and take short cuts through neighborhoods that I probably would never notice otherwise. The physical effects of exercising right after work really help me to leave my work behind, and give me a burst of energy for the rest of my day."

"Commuting by bike does take a little extra time and effort, but," says Jisa, "it's worth it not only for the benefits to your own physical and mental health, but the health of the planet. It's something you can be proud of every day."

*This column appeared in The Herald Sun in November 2005.*

# Ice puts focus on need for different kind of cities

Cafeteria conversation at work on January 31st revolved around the predicted ice storm. Bread, milk, and bottled water would be cleared off grocery store shelves by the time we left work that evening we all joked. We also guessed that the next day's news would be littered with images of cars skidding off the road.

It's not that Southerners can't drive in wintery conditions. Neither can the local transplants from New England or the midwest. No one can drive on ice.

And since no one can drive on ice, the answer is not to drive at all.

What we can do to prepare for the next ice storm is break away from our dependence on the automobile. The problem with giving up the car is that our communities are designed so that driving is necessary. Walking to the store is often not an option.

Since the 1950s, residential development in this country has revolved around the personal automobile. Because cars enable us to drive farther, our communities have been spreading. Look at growth patterns for any major city in the US for the past forty years, and you'll see a consistent pattern. Unless locked by geographic features (like Pittsburgh's rivers) or municipal decisions (like Portland, Oregon's growth belt), cities grow at the periphery. They expand. And Durham is no exception.

So, no one lives around the corner from the corner store anymore, and very few of us live around the corner from work.

The outskirts of town is where new neighborhoods go up. But while residential development sprawls, employment hubs like downtowns, universities, government buildings, and dense commercial districts remain the daily destinations for hundreds of thousands of drivers Triangle-wide. Research Triangle Park is the archetypal employment center – zoned for businesses only, every single one of the nearly 40,000 employees has to get into and out of RTP every week day. (Lest anyone thinks I'm pointing the finger at others, I'm one of those 40,000 traveling into RTP every day.)

The Triangle Transit Authority's buses serve the park, and DOT recently striped bike lanes on the freshly repaved Cornwallis Rd. But in an ice storm, neither buses nor bikes handle the roads any better than cars.

This growth at the periphery mindset is what drives big-box retail. Giant grocery stores and retail chains anchor parking lots larger than football fields, just waiting for us to drive to them. In fact, in some parking lots you get the feeling that you're out of place if you're not in a car. Try walking or riding your bike to Southpoint Mall. It's clear the expectation is that we drive to the store.

Not only do giant retail chains water down the flavor of business by making the suburbs of any town indistinguishable from any other (what Parisians are currently calling "banalization"), national chains drive locally owned hardware stores, fruit stands, and grocery co-ops out of business. And this means that our development patterns determine for us our transportation patterns – car dependent and subject to the weather.

Why can't Durham lead the effort to offer up another development model?

Ice is not the only reason to think about creating different kinds of cities. Even OPEC, the cartel of the largest oil exporting countries, finally admits that "peak oil" – the term reserved for the economic aftermath of a world in which oil production reaches a peak and then rapidly declines – could happen in the next decade.

Crippling ice storms give us a glimpse at what life after peak oil may look like if we don't start designing transportation around something other than the automobile. While many communities around the country are already making plans for the peak oil crisis, the Triangle is back to ground-zero designing a regional rail system.

Of course, anyone who's seen the movie *The Ice Storm* knows that not even trains can move safely through the frozen glaze, so regional rail is not the answer. But as long as we look for the one thing to deliver us from auto-topia, our future planning will be as stalled as a Camaro on I-40 in an ice storm. Regional rail is part of the answer; so is a more efficient bus network. So is mixed-use, high-density residential development in our existing employment hubs. So is a sidewalk and crosswalk infrastructure that accommodates wheelchairs and strollers.

Each city and county has a development review board, which can be more than just a rubber stamp on developer-submitted plans. Durham County Commissioner Becky Heron knows that, and that's why she's one of Durham's best advocates for smart development.

In addition to being ranked among the "Best Places to Live" and "Best Places to do Business," Durham's most recent honor is a spot among Forbes Magazine's December 2006 list of the top ten "Smartest Cities". If we're so smart, then we can figure out how to make Durham a more walkable community.

Walkable communities are safer communities. Whether a community is safe isn't always a measure of crime – a safe Durham is one where you can cross Roxboro Street without fearing for your life. A safe Durham is one where Duke Street and Gregson Street are no longer freeways running through the middle of neighborhoods.

A safe community is one in which getting to the store, running errands, caring for an elderly friend or parent, or getting to work isn't made impossible by the weather.

A walkable community is one in which during Triangle-wide ice storms, we can get to the food, firewood, or friendship we need to endure it.

*This column appeared in The Herald Sun in February 2007.*

The hardest working cyclists in Ottawa, Angelo Sarrazin and Allen Grier. (Ottawa, Canada)

# Ottawa pros offer advice

Feeling trapped inside by the cold weather? Are you taking a break from cycling until the spring thaw?

Winter cycling has an allure all its own, but to be sure it also has its challenges. I recently spent some time in Ontario and saw how truly dedicated cyclists make their way through the streets of Canada's frozen capital.

So, for some advice on cycling through the winter, I turn to the hardest working professional cyclists in Ottawa: the bike messengers. Like year round bike commuters, couriers have no choice when to ride. They ride every day they're working, and most of them are working every day.

The capital city's couriers offer four nuggets of advice to wintertime cyclists.

First, don't fall for thinking that knobby tires make good winter tires.

A lot of people think, "because of wintery slush on the roads that knobby tires are in order," says Crazy Dave, a long time Ottawa messenger. But knobbies won't help, he says. "The snow packs in between the knobs and actually makes it worse." Your traditional narrow road tires, or "slicks," actually cut through the snow and find pavement to grip.

Sure enough, as I glance around at the couriers' bikes congregating at the World Exchange Plaza, almost all of them are bear the slick road tires.

But the Triangle area is known more for its ice than snow, so which is the best for one of those glazed over days? Well, neither slicks nor knobbies are going to grip the ice. Studded tires are about the only things that work, but chances are if you need the studded tires, you don't need to be out on the roads.

Second, Dave "Rambo" Besharah suggests using fenders over your tires. Roads dry out more slowly in the winter, and Durham's greenways are often wet in the mornings. A nice set of fenders will keep your rear tire from slinging all that water on your back and your front tire from soaking your pants legs.

Planet Bike sells supposedly indestructible sets of shiny, polycarbonate mold-injected fenders for both mountain bike frames and road frames. They come with mud-flaps and all the hardware necessary to mount them on your bike. Or, you could take a more do-it-yourself approach, like Rambo. His fenders are pieced together from lengths of plastic, cut-up tubes, and a combination of duct and electrical tape. He's even gone so far as to wrap the stanchions of his suspension fork in tube rubber to keep the corrosive salty slush out.

Third, all the extra water on the roads will demand more time for maintenance if you want to keep that drivetrain running smoothly. But for many of us, bike maintenance is the last thing you want to do after a cold ride. The wheels will be wet, the frame freezing, the chain and cogs greasy. The risk is that if you don't put in the time to dry and lube the drivetrain, you're letting parts of your bike rust. And rust is the last thing you want to see developing on your precious ride.

Allen Grier, a self-identified rookie with just four years experience on the streets of Ottawa, says there's no way he's going to put in the time needed to take proper care of his nice bike during the winter. So, each winter he picks up a "beater" – a cheap bike that he converts to a single-speed and rides into the ground. Cheap frames are usually steel or chromoly, both of which are fond of rust. With no maintenance, a beater will do well to last one winter in Ottawa; there's just so much salt a bottom bracket can withstand before cracking.

Fourth, whether you pick up a "beater" or not, make your winter bike a single-speed. Grier's not the only one riding with just one gear in the rear – most of the couriers' trusty steeds are single speeds.

And many of them are fixed gears.

Even if you're not adverse to the cold, chances are you won't be able to spend as much time riding in February as you can in June. Riding a single speed allows you to get in a pretty intense workout in a shorter period of time. Because a fixed gear bike won't let you coast, riding one of these cadence masters offers the most return for time spent on the bike. And as Angelo Sarrazin, an eight-year veteran of Ottawa's streets, reminds me, "if the brake cables rust through and snap, you've still got brakes on a fixed gear."

*This column appeared in The Herald Sun in February 2006.*

# Taking on toxins is worth it

S ome winter mornings, while riding in Cornwallis Road's new bike lanes, I can smell Counter Culture Coffee roasting those fairly traded coffee beans two or more miles to the south. The same still air that pools summertime ozone over the region's largest employment hub wafts the unique smell of coffee beans expanding in heat, releasing their caffeinated oils. Whenever I ride through one of those invisible, aromatic clouds, I breathe deeply.

Problem is, I can also smell the exhaust from the surrounding cars at every intersection.

No doubt, on-road cyclists are more vulnerable to their environments than drivers. It's not just that we're naked next to multi-ton hunks of steel hurtling past us (in either direction) at deadly speeds and proximities too close for comfort, but we're also exposed to the gases of the landscape. Any winter bike commuter has observed that cold air appears to keep exhaust fumes closer to the ground. Which means that while waiting at each red light, we're treated to a special dose of carbon monoxide, sulfur dioxide, and nitrogen dioxide, complete with that lovely smell (except for those biodiesel converts; then we're tricked into thinking someone is cooking up French fries nearby).

Summertime cyclists know to check the ozone forecast just like the weather forecast. Summer ozone concentrations in NC can reach toxic levels, and athletes are sometimes advised not to engage in rigorous cardiovascular activity on those days.

So, I started wondering whether biking is actually an unhealthy thing to do. I mean, coasting up to each intersection, it sure feels like I'm breathing in more car exhaust than when I'm a passenger in a car. So who better to ask than public health specialists?

Doctoral students at UNC's School of Public Health and scientists at the National Institute of Environmental Health Sciences help tackle these questions – Do cyclists have any reason to worry about what we're breathing in on our (supposedly healthy) ways to work? And if so, which is the greater health risk – the colorless, odorless ozone in the summer or the pungent, cloudy exhaust fumes in the winter?

Dave Love says that "cycling is a balance of risks." Love, a PhD candidate in UNC's School of Public Health, says that "the risk of getting into an accident is probably the most serious risk a cyclist faces. But lets say you are a careful biker, then another one to consider is your concern about taking deep breaths of exhaust during exercise. You are breathing more deeply and faster than drivers, so you are getting exposed to more exhaust and ozone. But, to look on the bright side, our urban air quality is probably better than 150 years ago!"

While a cyclist might be breathing in more noxious gases than automobile drivers, it's worth pointing out that a car doesn't protect drivers from those gases. Since a car's air-conditioning and heating intake filters cannot filter out volatile organic compounds like benzene, drivers are exposed to the same gases as cyclists. At best, automobiles' ventilation systems only disguise the smell of roadways by filtering the air through activated charcoal filters.

NIEHS scientist and avid cyclist Jerry Phelps says that, from his experience, the amount of air pollution from car exhaust probably doesn't change from one season to the next. It's more visible in the winter because the air is colder and drier. The water vapor mixed in with car exhaust is what we're able to see leaking from the tailpipe. The same amount of exhaust hangs near the ground behind cars in the summer too, but since humidity levels are generally higher in the summer months, we just can't see it.

Whether there's more exhaust in the winter or not, there's still the question of what those gases are doing to our lungs. "It's likely that the health benefits of increased physical activity are greater than the risks incurred because of increased exposure to air pollution," says Audrey de Nazelle, also a doctoral student in UNC's School Of Public Health. "But, if you have respiratory problems to start out with, then it's another story."

People with asthma are much more sensitive to particulate matter and toxic gases, which is why asthma sufferers are warned about the ozone levels in the summer.

Stephanie J. London, M.D., a senior investigator in the epidemiology branch and laboratory of respiratory biology at NIEHS agrees with Nazelle. "It's hard to say whether ozone or exhaust fumes are worse since both are basically bad. And even though you would probably breathe more ozone riding your bike than traveling in a car, the exercise will probably outweigh the negative effects."

Reading Lance Armstrong's *It's Not About the Bike*, you learn two things. First, Armstrong is a lucky guy. The lottery of life granted him the abnormal lung capacity and the muscular distribution to become a world-class athlete. And second, the body's ability to heal itself is the most powerful, restorative advantage we have when fighting disease. Armstrong couldn't have beaten testicular cancer without chemotherapy, but neither could he have recovered from the brutalized depths of chemotherapy without a resilient, toned body. The medical community surrounding Armstrong agrees that he recovered from cancer as well as he did because he is an athlete.

Exercise enhances the body's ability to repair itself. Cardiovascular activity strengthens the immune system, and since both drivers and cyclists are exposed to the same toxins, the cyclists may come out better in the long run. In short, people who exercise have bodies that are better able to process the toxins we all take in.

*This column appeared in The Herald Sun in March 2007.*

Roll Your Own and Save Your Roll (Durham, NC)

# Driving the kids with a bicycle

Four days a week, Teddy Salazar takes his son Theo to school just like most parents. Instead of a car seat, however, Theo rides in a trailer towed behind Salazar's bicycle. Weaving around potholes and climbing hills along four miles of west Durham's streets, Salazar tows his son to and from pre-school. Hard work though it may be for Salazar, "it's actually lots of fun," he says.

"We wave to people on their porches on Carroll Street. We get all sorts of comment like, 'Look at that!' or 'How cute!' when we ride by Duke. It's really easy to stop for coffee, a snack or a potty break.

It's a long commute after all."

Theo rides in a Burley Solo, a single seat trailer crafted by one of three major bike trailer designers. Burley joins bicycle manufacturers Giant and Trek to offer trailers that are designed specifically for hauling children.

Salazar and his wife Sarah chose the Solo because its seat doesn't push the helmet forward over Theo's face when he sits back, buckled-in. The Solo attaches to the quick-release skewer of Salazar's rear wheel. And aside from keeping their speed under 15mph, the trailer seems stable enough not to require the cyclist to do anything special, says Salazar.

On my ride home from work one October evening, I ran into Reuben Stob along the American Tobacco Trail. Behind him, his son Arie was singing and bobbing along in a Burley D'Lite. Stob said he had just moved to Durham from Lithuania and used the trailer to carry his son home from daycare.

Later that same evening, I stopped Anga Pohlers on Erwin Rd to ask her about her trailer. Even before Erwin Rd was repaved and striped with bike lanes between the Duke Hospital and Ninth St, Erwin was wide enough to ride with a trailer behind, Pohlers said.

Aside from variations in color, the trailers all looked the same to me. So, I stopped by The Bicycle Chain for some help understanding the differences. Chris Phillips walked me through two of models they had in the store.

First up is the Trek Doodlebug, a lightweight aluminum alloy trailer ($280). It holds up to 100lbs, and comes equipped with two seats. Each seat has a "three-point harness with one point between the legs and shoulder straps over each shoulder," says Phillips.

"If you're going on a picnic, going to the store or to the neighborhood pool," adds Phillips, "there are small internal side pockets and storage space behind the seat."

Salazar's goal is to make Theo comfortable. "Parents who want to try towing their kids should be aware that" the kids will closer to the road – something to think about in summer heat – and closer to automobile wheels – something to think about in wet or dusty conditions.

On warm sunny days, the mesh covering that comes stock with the Solo or Doodlebug will suffice, but Salazar says he rolls down the Solo's plastic shell for rainy or windy days. The rain fly costs extra on the Doodlebug.

The Doodlebug, like most trailers mounts to the rear axle of the bike. It comes with a longer replacement skewer for the rear wheel; the new skewer holds the rear wheel of the bike in place and connects to the ball-and-socket joint that tows the trailer.

The ball-and-socket hitch design allows the trailer to pivot at most any angle so that the bike can move laterally independent of the trailer. Many parents choose to use trailers over bike-mounted child seats, says Phillips, since the trailer won't be affected if the cyclist loses balance.

The Burley D'Lite ($450) has a few safety features the Doodlebug lacks. It comes standard with bars on the trailer's sides that deflect trees or bollards around the trailer's wheels. If you've misjudged the the width of a trail's entrance, you might appreciate those bars. There's an integrated rain fly, a parking brake, and a unique hitch-mount design that doesn't require you to replace your skewer. The hitch clamps to bike's chainstay instead. For storage, the D'Lite also folds down smaller than Doodlebug.

Tim Griffin, a research fellow in Duke's Bioengineering lab and a member of the Bicycle and Pedestrian Advisory Commission, tows his two daughters in a Burley D'Lite.

"I've found that drivers are pretty considerate when you have a bike carrier," says Griffin. "In fact, the first morning I took the carrier to work with me cars were giving me wide clearance."

Other considerations for first time trailer haulers are the extended turning radius and the additional width that trailers add. For being seen on the road, each trailer comes with an orange flag, "but we also recommend blinkie lights if you'll be riding after dark," says Phillips.

Salazar recommends taking it to the store for hauling groceries or running some other errand first. Before strapping more precious cargo in those seats, "find out how long it takes to clear an intersection, what stopping is like or going up hill. There's a strange rubber band effect when trying to accelerate fast."

All of the people interviewed for this article also noted that they found their trailers through either Craigslist or the local newspaper's classified ads.

*This column appeared in The Herald Sun in December 2007.*

# Lanes do their job

Just two weeks ago, Main Street was one-way through downtown Durham. City officials closed the street Saturday and reopened it for traffic going in both directions. How do drivers know the difference?

City leaders ceremoniously proclaimed its transformation from the stage at Durham Rising, the party celebrating downtown's rebirth. Several newspaper articles and TV news broadcasts have mentioned it. Maps of downtown Durham will be redrawn at some point.

But many people will simply discover that Main Street is now a two-way street when they drive downtown and see the fresh yellow double line separating the lanes.

Lines on the road serve a purpose.

The yellow and white strips of reflective paint that city and state governments use on asphalt help to guide traffic. Drivers respond well to these guidelines, and that's exactly why there are lanes to facilitate the safe flow of traffic. We live (and drive) in an era when competition for drivers' attention revolves around anything but keeping the driver's eyes on the road. Cell phones, iPods, DVD players, and even video games have found a home inside automobiles. Lanes assist drivers whose attention may be split between Gnarls Barkley on the radio, Mortal Kombat in the back seat, a dentist on the other end of the phone and traffic.

Bike lanes do the same thing for drivers and cyclists that other lanes do. They guide all vehicles into predictable places on the road so that each person can safely go where she or he needs to go. The Pedestrian and Bicycling Information Center at UNC-Chapel Hill defines bike lanes as "a portion of the roadway which has been designated by striping , signing and pavement marking for the preferential or exclusive use by bicyclists."

By carving out a dedicated space on the road for bicycles, bike lanes remind drivers that they share the road with all different kinds of vehicles. As Nancy Gallman of Durham put it, "bike lanes create the expectation that bikes will be on the road, even if they aren't there right now." They train drivers to expect cyclists, and they welcome cyclists onto the road.

Bike lanes are critical for creating a bike-friendly community in one more way — they calm traffic. A typical outer lane is 14-feet wide. A 14-foot outer lane looks pretty wide, and traffic engineers know that drivers speed on wide roads. A 10-foot outer lane, however, looks a lot more narrow, and drivers naturally (if not subconsciously) drive more slowly. It simply requires more concentration to keep your car in your lane if your lane is narrow.

We can reduce outer-lane width to ten feet by using the remaining four feet for a bike lane. The American Association of State Highway and Transportation Officials sets their minimum bike lane width at four feet. Those four feet have to be asphalt — the bike lane can't push cyclists into the gutter. Nor would a well-designed bike lane be painted next to parked cars where cyclists would be forced to ride in the "door zone".

Granted, there are many examples of poorly designed bike lanes, some of which make riding more dangerous for cyclists than it would be without a bike lane. Just look at Duke University's Campus Drive bike lane for a local example. But poorly designed bike lanes are unsafe because they are poorly designed.

Further, cyclists are permitted full use of the road in North Carolina. If the bike lane is unsafe — because of gravel, pot holes, or any other reason — then cyclists are free to move out of it. Cyclists, like drivers, are expected to choose the safest means of travel.

Well-designed bike lanes foster safe riding; they do this best when bike lanes are part of a larger network of safe roads and greenways. Durham's new bike plan is a master plan for how Durham can use bike lanes safely and effectively. When designing them, let's make sure they go somewhere and they are safe, because cyclists are likely to use bike lanes when they connect to neighborhoods, workplaces, and recreation centers.

As a recent *Herald-Sun* editorial noted, Durham will see more cyclists hit the streets as gas prices continue to rise. The most important thing the city and county can do to foster Durham's growing bike community is to adopt design standards that take cyclists into consideration when designing and maintaining all roads.

*This piece ran as an Op-Ed in the Sunday edition of The Herald Sun, July 8th, 2007.*

# Road rules apply to bikes as well as driver

If le Tour de France inspired you to take a bike out for a spin, you're not alone. The bike industry has reported sales booms in previous Julys... those when Lance won the Tour. This year's race was just as inspiring, particularly in the mountain stages. It's always impressive to watch riders climb a hill faster than I could cruise down it.

The hill on Mt. Sinai Road isn't exactly Alpe d' Huez, but if you ride with a pack of fellow cyclists like the those in the Durham Cycle Center's weekly Tuesday ride, you might just feel like part of the peloton.

The biggest difference, however, between le Tour de France and your weekend tour of the Triangle will be traffic. Le Tour may be a tough bike ride, but for three weeks those riders don't have to put up with motorists. Apart from the support wagons and motorcycle-mounted cameras, they have the roads entirely to themselves.

We, however, share the road. We share it with vehicles much heavier than our bikes, and we're fairly vulnerable when out there riding. There are no race officials cordoning off the road ahead for us, so our personal safety is our own responsibility. Riding your bike on the road isn't all that tricky, because most safety is just common sense.

Bicycles are classified by state and municipal laws as vehicles. This means two important things: first, their proper place is on the road. Second, bikes are subject to traffic laws just like any other vehicle. Plainly, to get from here to there on a bike, you should be riding on the road–not on a sidewalk. In fact, Durham's city ordinances require any cyclists older than 12 to ride in the road.

The safest place to ride in the road is on the right hand side of the lane. Durham cyclist David Boynton describes his lane position as "out in the road with the right side of the handlebar on the line." Riding here allows cars the chance to pass when it's clear and it also allows the rider some room to maneuver around potholes and lane debris.

Even though many new cyclists are uncomfortable turning their backs to the traffic, riding with the flow of traffic is far safer than riding against it. And with time, it'll feel more natural.

Since most accidents (in cars or on bikes) happen at intersections, keep a careful eye out at stop signs, traffic lights, and even driveways. Most accidents result when one person just doesn't see the other. On your bike, ride predictably and try to be cognizant of how visible to others you are. Bright clothing or blinking lights may help.

Most of us cyclists are also drivers. So when you trade the handlebars for a steering wheel and you encounter a cyclist on the road, remember what it's like to be that cyclist. Drivers interact with cyclists best when they treat the bike as just another vehicle on the road.

When passing a bicycle, it's courteous to give the rider as wide a berth as you would a car. The NC DMV's driver's manual states that "drivers wishing to pass a bicyclist may do so only when there is abundant clearance and no oncoming traffic is in the opposing lane. When passing a bicyclist, always remember the bicyclist is entitled to the use of the full lane." So, even though a bike takes up less room than a car, the cyclist has a right to the lane and may need extra room to dodge a pothole.

Contrary to popular belief, the DMV does not recommend tapping your horn to alert the cyclist of your presence. As you approach a bike from behind, most cyclists are already aware that you're there (even though they may not give any indication).

I've heard from more than one reader of this column that as

drivers they are often frustrated when they encounter a group of bikers riding together and crowding the road. This happens more often on the rural roads surrounding the Triangle than the city streets. While there's certainly a social component to any group ride, cyclists also ride in groups for better visibility and thus greater safety.

So if you encounter a peloton on 751 down by Lake Jordan, just be patient. They'll soon fall in line on the right hand side of the road, and you'll be on your way.

*This column appeared in The Herald Sun in July 2005.*

# Why share the road?

If you haven't heard, the state of North Carolina just issued new "Share the Road" license plates. For $30 annually, cyclists who drive can show their fondness of two wheels even while in their car. And if talk in the local cycling community is right, these new license tags couldn't have come at a better time.

In June, *The Herald Sun* reported that Durham cyclist Drew Cummings was hit and seriously injured while riding to Pittsboro. Whether it was an accidental or intentional hit and run, the driver fled the scene and has yet to be identified.

Greg Sousa reports on a local cycling listserv that he was run off the road on his way to work one morning in July. And Douglas Woolcock says that someone in a passing car threw a fast-food cup at him while he was cycling down 9th Street. Both are skeptical that these encounters were accidents since both incidents involved a passenger in the car raising a middle finger out the window.

What's going on here? Are the rising temperatures interfering with our sense of compassion? Do rising gas prices make it more difficult for motorists to show patience on the road? Do the summer swarms of cyclists upset all drivers?

A reader of this column, who wishes to remain anonymous, opines that some motorists are reluctant to share the road with cyclists who defiantly disregard traffic laws. Cyclists running red lights and stop signs are just a few of the anarchic affairs he's irritated by. And, he thinks, these small acts of rebellion may be igniting a territorial instinct in other drivers.

He may be right. I've listened to radicals on both sides of this issue. To hear some motorists talk about the perceived arrogance of cyclists, you'd think that sharing lane space with a bicycle offends them deeply. To hear some cyclists talk about the perceived arrogance of drivers, you'd think every car with which they share the road puts their life as well as national security in danger.

But vigilante justice, whether it's a motorist chasing down an errant cyclist or a cyclist brandishing a U-lock as a weapon, is also against the law. More than illegal, it's shameful behavior.

Thinking in extremes, leaves us prone to confrontation. It locks motorists and cyclists in a turf battle over space on the road, and no one wins a battle like this.

Roadways are dangerous places simply by virtue of the fact that they are filled with independently moving machines – each traveling with enough speed to harm the delicate human body. Cars and bikes can mingle together safely, but only if we leave our attitudes out of the mix.

Let's not let our tempers rise as high as the temperature. Rather than polarize the road, let's share it calmly and safely.

*This column appeared in The Herald Sun in August 2005.*

Just north of the Edison Johnson Center, near the Ellerbee Creek Trail (Durham, NC)

# Drivers must always be attentive and responsible

*Herald Sun* article this past week described a hit-and-run by saying, "a recent Duke University graduate was critically injured when she was hit by a car late Friday on South LaSalle Street near McQueen Drive, according to police. The vehicle left the scene without stopping, police said."

One from a few months ago, describing an altogether different incident, says that "two women walking next to Kingston Drive were injured when a teenage driver left the road and hit them Friday afternoon." A later article concerning the same incident says that "a motorist ran off a road and struck two pedestrians Friday afternoon."

There's an important difference between saying that a pedestrian was hit by a car and saying that a driver ran off the road and struck pedestrians.

One way describes a world where accidents are the products of inanimate objects attacking innocent people. The other way makes it clear that those dangerous, inanimate objects are themselves driven by people too.

The language we use to describe accidents matters. If we go through life describing all accidents as incidents when inanimate objects unexplainably hurt people, then the world becomes a much scarier place. This careless use of language can contribute to the fear mongering of which the media is perpetually accused. The world described in this way is scarier, in part, because there is no responsibility and, therefore, no solution to the problems.

No one seriously defends the claim that we're not responsible for anything we do unintentionally. And so it goes with driving. Just because there are circumstances beyond our control doesn't mean we're absolved from all responsibility.

But accidents happen, you say. Not every accident is someone's fault, you're thinking. And I agree. But as drivers, if we think that just because our vehicles weigh so much and extend so far beyond our reach that we aren't responsible for what happens as a result of our driving, then we need to rethink what it means to drive a car.

Whether or not a driver involved in an accident is held legally responsible, it's still the case that someone was driving the car when the accident happened. To tell the story without the driver is to dehumanize the incident.

Why take the human element out of the narrative? If no one is responsible, then who's driving the cars?

If we take the human out of the vehicle, then we take responsibility away from the driver. And if we habitually describe these incidents with no one responsible, then we start thinking of accidents as inevitable.

We don't usually choose to have accidents, but we all make bad choices that make accidents more likely. If we choose to speed, then we're choosing to make our streets more dangerous for ourselves and for cyclists and pedestrians. Speeding, like driving drunk – or driving while on the cell phone, or while adjusting the radio, or while putting on makeup, or while changing clothes, or while eating – affects our ability to avoid accidents. And while drivers of Escalades, Expeditions, and Tahoes have at least an illusion of security, those of us on two wheels don't have even that.

In order to ride bicycles safely in traffic, cyclists need to recognize that the laws of physics are immutable. Just because a 3-ton vehicle shouldn't be passing through the crosswalk, much less at 45 mph, doesn't mean it's able to stop in a matter of feet. Just because a bus shouldn't be driving in the bike lane doesn't mean that it's going

Phillip Barron

to move out of your way.

Only if we're all responsible for our vehicles is there a solution. More attentive driving, less electronic media distracting drivers, less alcohol intoxicating drivers, more driver (and cyclist and pedestrian) education are all changes that could make a difference in a world where drivers are responsible for their vehicles. These changes wouldn't make any difference in a world where cars simply careen out of control and strike pedestrians and cyclists.

I challenge the media to describe incidents more accurately. I also challenge cyclists, pedestrians, and especially drivers to take more responsibility for our vehicles.

*This column appeared in The Herald Sun in October 2006.*

# Ride of Silence to speak loudly about bike safety

The Ride of Silence on Wednesday will be the loudest statement of the year on bicycle safety and it will be spoken without a word.

The Ride of Silence is a Triangle-wide event, beginning at the Triangle Life Science Center (the former EPA building) at the corner of Alexander Drive and N.C. 54 in Research Triangle Park.

The second annual ride is for cyclists of all abilities and levels of experience. After a brief moment of silence and stillness, the assembled riders will take to the streets in hushed solemnity, proceeding slowly – using only hand signals for necessary communication – down Alexander Drive, completing a 5-mile loop through RTP, and returning to the Triangle Life Science Center. This is a no-drop ride.

The Ride of Silence honors and remembers cyclists who have been injured or killed on public roads. The goal is to raise the awareness of motorists, cyclists, law enforcement, and city officials that there's more work to do to share the road.

The Ride of Silence is bigger than the Triangle. The local event is one of more than 190 concurrent events in the United States. Also on Wednesday, eight other countries will host silent processions, each in honor of cyclists who have died or been injured will riding.

The Ride of Silence is a simple, grassroots event. "There is no brochure, no sponsors, no registration fees and no T-shirt," say event organizers Blanche and Larry Dean.

"The Ride of Silence," says Pete Schubert, Durham Bicycle and Pedestrian Advisory Commission member, "reminds us of the ultimate cost to cyclists when drivers fail to pay attention, ignore the rules of the road, disobey traffic laws, are not courteous, or otherwise do not respect their fellow drivers. We all know, in bike-motor vehicle collisions, the cyclist usually loses – sometimes his or her life – while the motorist usually lives to regret his or her experience."

The Ride of Silence is focused on safety. The organizers require that all participants wear helmets. Since the ride will finish at or just after dark, bring lights (headlight and taillight) if you plan to ride home.

The Ride of Silence has new significance this year for IBM employee Brian Carver. He has a hard time forgetting the moment of impact, when he crashed into the car window, bouncing off and landing on the road.

"I try to keep my head clear and forget that each car that passes next to me can snuff me out in a second. All it takes is one moment away from the road to text message your friends and the next moment you're explaining to a cop why you killed that rather obvious cyclist in the bike lane," says Carver, recalling the story of a cyclist killed in Colorado earlier this year.

"It took a long time for me to get the courage to ride again," Carver adds.

The Ride of Silence takes place this year at a time when soaring gas prices are encouraging some commuters to look for alternatives to driving and beautiful spring weather is turning some of those commuters to cycling. "We all must learn how to share the road and then practice safe driving every time we take to the road," Schubert says.

The Ride of Silence will leave the Triangle Life Science Center parking lot promptly at 7 p.m. "Cyclists should arrive early enough to air up their tires and participate in a moment of silence before the ride," Blanche Dean advises. "Daylight permitting, a second loop may be ridden."

The Ride of Silence is a reminder that motorists and cyclists will always co-exist on the road. Whether we co-exist safely is up to us.

*This column appeared in The Herald Sun in May 2006.*

# Women's biking group offers fun, support

S usan Crosjean of Raleigh practices "popping" her front wheel off the ground again and again. Once she's comfortable with the move, she aims her bike at a tightly packed row of logs, each 12 inches in diameter. Riding toward them, she gathers speed. She's cheered on by her friends and encouraged by spotters, who are there just in case.

She lifts her front wheel, then the rear, and rolls gracefully over the stunt.

I ask later whether she's ever cleared that stunt before. "Never," she says, "but I don't let anything stand in my way. I do it again and again until I get it."

This is a typical evening for the women of GRID.

Just over a year old and more than 100 members deep, GRID — Girlz Riding in Dirt — is a Trianglewide, all-women's mountain bike club. Last week, GRID founder Peggy Dodge let me tag along at Lake Crabtree County Park with 10 of the club's members.

I've never ridden with a more excitable bunch. Riding through the woods, you'll hear just as many "Yahoo!" shouts as supportive words. This group hits the trails to have fun.

Experience levels among GRID's members run the gamut, from newbies to racers.

Right now, "GRID primarily caters to the less-experienced crowd and intermediate riders," Dodge says. "Let's face it, for a beginning rider the trail can be very pushy and intimidating." Membership benefits include "no-drop rides, weekly mailings, bike maintenance and skills clinics, group trips and a great time! It's very social."

Lisa Schell of Cary adds another benefit: "It's nice to be around people who understand it's OK to have three bikes."

Encouraging riders like Crosjean to improve their skills in a noncompetitive, friendly, confidence-building environment is exactly what GRID specializes in.

Many of GRID's riders started mountain biking within the last three years and choose to ride with the club to develop technique. Paula Frost of Holly Springs sports the new woman-specific Specialized Stumpjumper. "Peggy got me into mountain biking," she says. "She's very positive; a good teacher." Three years and four bikes later, Frost says she's riding 'til she's 50.

"What? I'm not stopping at 50," shouts Schell.

Amaris Guardiola, a hard-tail rider from Graham, has been mountain biking since 1996. Echoing a sentiment I heard repeatedly that evening, Guardiola says she used to ride alone, but started riding with GRID for the companionship.

"Everyone's just so encouraging," she said.

Schell says her riding improved after her first GRID ride. She raises her voice to announce, "Hey Peggy! Two days in a row, I didn't fall!"

Yeah... I was the only one who tumbled on the trail Tuesday night.

The guys can join in the fun on any of GRID's co-ed rides, but Dodge keeps the club focused on women. "I actually established GRID for selfish reasons... I wanted to ride with other women and not just the boys who were so much stronger and more skilled than me," she told me ahead of time. "Women are more cautious while men approach their riding more aggressively, facing the consequences later."

If I'd listened, maybe I wouldn't have ended up face down on a switchback.

Phillip Barron

Dodge would also like to see GRID expand by developing a team component to the club, "to have an individual who can establish a race program and build membership by recruiting more advanced riders."

Back at the trailhead, we stand around swapping stories, discussing the benefits of clipless pedals and bashguards, and sharing riding techniques. Just like any other group bike ride, the conversation inevitably turns to pizza. The camaraderie never stops.

*This column appeared in The Herald Sun in May 2005.*

# Have no fear, cyclists, Officer BMX is on the job

Riding along the American Tobacco Trail on my way home from work, I come up behind another bicyclist. I slow down to say hello, as I always do.

My fellow biker assertively tells me to slow down, to pull over and that he is a cop.

"Of course, Officer," I say, unlocking my shoe from the pedal and squeezing the brakes a little harder. When we both stop conveniently at an intersection, I look more closely at the arresting officer: a young boy, no more than 9 years old.

"I read in the paper that the Durham police are putting more cops on bikes this year," I say.

Reading either the skeptical look on my face or my willingness to play along, he shows off his radio, which validates his ability to protect and serve. It's the hand-held mouthpiece to a CB radio with its coiled wire tied to the handlebars of his BMX bike.

"Seen any trouble on your ride today?" he asks me.

"No, not yet, but I could use some help crossing this intersection." Riding his own bike nearby, the cop's older brother — I mean superior officer — smiles at the two of us.

Like cops in the movies do, Officer BMX is eyeballing me — with a squint no less. Kids are fascinated by gadgets, and he's taking in the utilitarian nature of my gear: shoes that lock into the pedals, a rubber band around my right ankle to keep my pants cuffs out of the greasy crank, a rack holding my sandals and blinking tail light, a brightly colored shoulder bag with reflective tape and most importantly, my helmet.

Officer BMX happily complies, escorting me through the intersection once he determines the coast is clear.

"Did you respond to any calls today, any trouble in the neighborhood?" I ask him.

"Yeah, a girl had a bike accident earlier. I had to help her fix her bike. It's been quiet since then," he replied.

On the other side of the road, I thank him for helping me across the street and for keeping this route safe for me and for other cyclists.

As I click into my pedals and begin to pull away, I think he might ride with me. Instead, he turns around and rides back through the intersection. I guess he can't stray too far from home, I mean, outside his jurisdiction.

*This column appeared in The Herald Sun in April 2005.*

DURHAM ENGLAND
4119 Miles

ARUSHA TANZANIA
7839 Miles

KOSTROMA RUSSIA
5302 Miles

TOYAMA JAPAN
7090 Miles

DURHAM'S
SISTER CITIES

Durham Central Park (Durham, NC)

# Section III: A World of Cycling

The bicycle is the most civilized conveyance known to man. Other forms of transport grow daily more nightmarish.

Iris Murdoch, *The Red and the Green*

Shopping by bike (Buenos Aires, Argentina)

# World needs your old bicycles

In Ghana, the availability of a reliable bicycle turns a 2 hour walk to school into a 25 minute ride.

In Guatemala, it means that someone who previously could not carry their wares to a market now has a way.

In Namibia, where specially equipped bicycles become pedal-powered ambulances, it can be the difference between life and death.

"Bikes empower people to change their lives," says Merywen Wigley. As an HIV/AIDS professional working in international health, Wigley has witnessed personally the difference two wheels can make.

An avid cyclist before ever stepping foot in Africa, she was moved by seeing healthcare workers traversing rural Zambia by bike to deliver medications and check on patients.

She learned that many communities in the developing world receive their bicycles as donations, salvaged castaways from countries like the United States. Since 2002, Wigley has volunteered with Bikes for the World.

According to their website, Bikes for the World's central mission is to collect unwanted bicycles and related material in the United States and deliver it at low cost to community development programs assisting the poor in developing countries or in the Washington DC metropolitan area. As much as possible, Bikes for the World (BFW) uses the donated bicycles to help set-up self-sustaining bicycle repair operations which can make enough money to pay the shipping costs for subsequent container shipments of donated bicycles. Since 1995, BFW shipped more than 30,000 bikes overseas. Wigley and other Durham residents are starting a new Triangle chapter.

On Saturday, March 29th, local BFW volunteers will see how many bicycles they can pack into a 24-foot UHaul. They hope to get at least 200.

To do that, they need your help.

That Saturday is a Triangle-wide collection drive. In a parking lot in Research Triangle Park, volunteers will be receiving your donations, making a few mechanical adjustments to each bike for more compact shipping, and loading the bikes onto a truck bound for

Washington, DC. From there, BFW will load the cycles into a shipping container bound for either Africa or Latin America.

Road bikes, mountain bikes, kids' bikes, or adult bikes all make great donations. BFW asks that you please donate whole bikes rather than parts and frames. But a bike with flat tires, broken cables, or a rusty chain is fine. "As long as everything on the bike turns, we can use it," Dan Gatti explains.

"We also ask for a $10 donation with each bike to offset the cost of shipping." It costs $20 to get a bike from the collection point to the community in the developing world. "Bikes for the World pays half, and we ask the folks who donate a bike to pay the other half," Magill says.

"Besides," says Marcus Rogers, "anyone who has ever boxed and shipped their own bike knows that $10 is a deal."

Jack Warman, a member of the Durham Bicycle and Pedestrian Advisory Committee, decided to get involved with BFW after hearing a recent BBC radio-documentary on the Bicycle Empowerment Network in Namibia. "Through groups like BFW," says Warman, "you can take something that we, who are extraordinarily spoiled, would throw away and turn it into something that can change someone's life."

Emily Dings agrees. "Bikes have been a great avenue for me to find meaningful activities, and this seems like another one of those meaningful activities," she says.

Meaningfulness also ruled the day in a recent test of creative mettle.

Software giant Google and bicycle component manufacturer Shimano teamed up to sponsor a contest challenging inventors to create the next radical shift in cycling technology. Innovate or Die, the contest's name a harbinger of the high stakes on inventiveness in the age of global climate change, drew entries that range the spectrum from the next super-light frame material to the successor to the derailleur.

The winner, though, is simpler. It's a bike that stores water and filters it while you pedal.

That such a unpretentious, utilitarian bike won this international contest of ingenuity serves as a reminder that bicycles are tools as much as they are toys. They are vehicles with a long history of liberation through simplicity.

As Warman muses, "bicycles can change the world."

*This column appeared in The Herald Sun in February 2008.*

# Women's Liberation Through Cycling

F or many, the nineties were a time of political advancement and financial success. The economy was doing well, failed policies from previous administrations were being turned back, manufacturing was on the increase, and progress was the buzz-word in board rooms and parlors.

This national excitement had something, more than a little, to do with the fact that the 1890s were also the height of the bicycle boom in the United States. In 1897 alone, approximately three hundred manufacturers in the US sold more two million bicycles, doubling production from the previous year.

The bicycle had been invented only thirty years earlier, and the constant stream of improvements to its design was a celebrated sign of progress. The bicycle's adoption by women of the era made the bicycle literally and metaphorically a vehicle of social change.

In the 1930s, local newspaper columnist Wyatt T. Dixon wrote a few articles reflecting on bicycles' popularity in 1887. B.L. Duke and Company's furniture store rented high wheelers (the kind of bikes with a front wheel nearly as tall as the rider and much smaller rear wheel) for ten cents an hour. If you could afford it, renting bicycles and learning to ride the wobbly contraptions was a popular form of entertainment in 1887. Watching the cyclists fall off the bikes was equally entertaining for the crowd that formed every weekend.

Cycling, as Dixon reports it, was a man's activity.

Between 1887 and 1890, the number of cyclists in the US doubled. "The vast majority of new purchasers, many of whom were women, favored the new 'safety bicycle,'" says David Herlihy in *Bicycle*. The safety bicycle resembles what we now think of as a bicycle: two wheels of equal size with a chain-driven rear axle and lever-operated brakes. Its invention and mass production propelled cycling's popularity.

In a photograph dating to roughly 1895, young Durhamite Mamie Dowd poses proudly with an Overman Victoria bicycle. The Victoria, Overman's drop frame woman's model, was a fixed gear safety bicycle outfitted with solid rubber tires. According to The Smithsonian Institution, "the drop frame bicycle was developed so that women could ride while wearing a long skirt. It's adoption greatly increased the popularity of the bicycle, and helped make cycling a popular sport for women, as well as, a means of transportation."

Peter Zheutlin echoes the point Mamie Dowd claims to have been the first woman in Durham to own a bicycle. Photo courtesy of Milo Pyne. in his biography of Annie Londonderry, the first woman to bicycle around the world; "a woman with a bicycle no longer had to depend on a man for transportation."

No wonder then that in 1896 Susan B. Anthony said that bicycling had done more than anything else to emancipate women.

Dowd claimed to be the first woman in Durham to own a bicycle, though the authenticity of her claim is challenged by another photograph. In the second, two men and a woman pose in front of the Durham Electric Lighting Company in 1890. The two men stand in suits and top hats, while the woman wears a Victorian dress and hat. Notably, she is sitting astride a bicycle. The photo itself is a celebration of two major innovations of the time: the bicycle as well as Durham's first electricity provider.

We know from accounts that conservatives of the time saw the bicycle as a symbol of unwelcome social change. While it was a celebrated technological innovation and an admirable source of amusement for men (and even boys), the bicycle's role in women's liberation kept it mired in controversy.

In his 1901 memoir, traditionalist James Battle Avirett reminisces antebellum values and derides the bicycle for ruining "the grace of woman's attractive movement." His comments parallel a June 6, 1895 article in Statesville's daily, The *Landmark*, which notes that while "the number of women who ride bicycles is growing with great rapidity... even in the best and prettiest of costumes, no woman looks dignified while riding a bicycle."

For conservatives, what was unwelcome about women cycling had as much to do with the resulting changes in women's clothing as it had to do with these so-called 'new women' traveling on their own.

Zheutlin explains that "cycling required a more practical, rational form of dress, and the large billowing skirts and corsets started to

give way to bloomers."

In short, when it came to women, "cycling, and the dress reform that accompanied it, challenged traditional gender norms," says Zheutlin.

In this photo dating to 1890, a woman sits astride a bicycle in front of Durham's first power plant.
Source: Photograph of the Durham Electric and Lighting Co., in Wyatt T. Dixon Papers, Rare Book, Manuscript, and Special Collections Library, Duke University, Durham, North Carolina.

Durham embraced the progress perhaps more easily than other cities its size. Women were working in tobacco factories as early as the 1880s, and local historian Jean

Phillip Barron

Anderson notes that in 1896 "continuing efforts toward independence" led Durham women to create their own literary and social clubs, splintering away from male-dominated groups.

A third photograph from the era, this one also from 1895, shows a young boy and girl straddling bicycles in the driveway of the Morehead House on Duke Street.

Despite its high cost, the bicycle's popularity transcended class. "Hundreds of thousands in the United States," says Youth's Companion magazine in the summer of 1896, "saved 'every spare penny' to buy a wheel," and to the detriment of other

Young cyclists pose with some of the first children's safety bicycles and pose in front of the Morehead house. ca.1895

Source: "Residence of Mrs. L.L. Morehead," Hand-book of Durham: a Brief and Accurate Description of a Prosperous and Growing Southern Manufacturing Town. Durham, N.C.: The Educator Company, 1895, p.76.

businesses. As these photographs of turn of the century Durham show, bicycle fever transcended age and race as well.

Although it is unclear whether Dowd was the first woman in Durham to have a bike, later in life she did become the first judge of Durham's Juvenile Court. Whether her bicycling days had anything to do with her later successful social reforms is up to you.

*This column appeared in The Herald Sun in March 2008.*

The acoustic dome at the Museum of Life and Science (Durham, NC)

# Cycling through Mexican streets is enjoyable

After asking at a taller de bicicletas (a bike shop) whether I could rent a bike, a mecanico leads me across the street to Pedro Martinez. Sr. Martinez is a former Olympic mountain biker who rents bikes and leads tours in Oaxaca, Mexico.

His office is small, just big enough for a counter, ten bikes to hang tightly against the wall, and shelves for helmets and cycling shoes. A collection of cycling jerseys hangs overhead, and inside the glass case that forms the counter are cassettes, pedals, hubs, and derailleurs. What available wall space is left is covered in poster-sized photographs of Martinez himself competing in races.

While Sr. Martinez is busy arranging a hiking tour with customers, his nephew Roberto invites me in. In the best Spanish I can muster, we joke about the pain of a long climb, about reaching down to click into the next easiest gear only to realize that you're already in it, and about the white-knuckles and big eyes of a sketchy descent. He tells me there is a 50 mile endurance mountain bike race on Sunday and invites me to race on a rented bike. I'm tempted but decline in favor of a ride through the streets of Oaxaca.

Sunday morning, I arrange to take a bike for two hours and ask about the local mountain bike scene. Roberto charges me 50 pesos (about $5.00) for a nice bike (a Giant Rincon), a pump and spare tube, tire levers, a lock, and a helmet.

Leaving the shop, I ride down la calle Aldama and turn south on JP Garcia. Although the sidewalks are crowded, traffic flows swiftly in the streets. Oaxaca is, like most developed areas, an auto-centric place. But bicycles fit right in with traffic here, and I never feel threatened by the buses, trucks, and taxis swirling around me. In fact, as I get more comfortable with the new traffic patterns, I realize that drivers around me seem to be more aware and respectful of bicyclists than I am used to.

I decide to ride the road up Monte Alban, a tight, steep road that leads to Zapotec ruins dating back to 100 AD. It's a grueling climb, but the views alone from the roadside make it worthwhile. Halfway up the road, I can see all of Oaxaca to the east. I snap a photograph in my mind and turn around.

Next I head north, riding the narrow one-way streets up to Chapultepec Highway. Although I see a few cyclists riding traditional road bikes, because of numerous speedbumps and the occasional cobblestone street, mountain bikes are the steeds of choice.

I reach the northern end of the city passing la Iglesia de Santo Domingo, a cathedral built between 1570 and 1608. Santo Domingo sits squarely inside the art district of Oaxaca, and I pass several cafés catering to gallery patrons. My two hours are coming to an end, so I turn back and begin riding southwest. On a bike, it's easy to navigate a city laid out in perfect square blocks, and I make my way to the Zócalo and the adjacent Alameda de León.

The Zócalo and Alameda de León are wide, auto-free pedestrian plazas where kids chase balloons, artists sell crafts, and musicians entertain day and night. I ride slowly through the crowds and notice several other cyclists also converging on the parks. These plazas are both the geographic and cultural focus of the city, drawing people to it. I feel as though I'm traveling against the natural flow of traffic as I leave the Zócalo and head south again for Aldama.

Roberto welcomes me back into the shade of the office and asks where I've ridden. I tell him that I now believe that a bicycle is the only way to see Oaxaca, and he agrees.

Out of curiosity, I ask whether he rents any single-speed mountain bikes. He laughs at the idea of riding a bike with only one gear in the mountains. I guess he needs to visit North Carolina.

*This column appeared in The Herald Sun in August 2005.*

# Hybrid car pitch a step backwards

September 14th marked the 108 year anniversary of the first pedestrian death at the hands of an automobile in the United States. On September 13th, 1899, Henry Bliss stepped from a streetcar on Central Park West, in New York, and was struck by a taxicab. He died of his injuries the next morning. The event was reported on the front page of the New York Times.

In 2005 alone, 39,000 automobile crashes in the United States accounted for 43,000 deaths.

Given the anniversary of Bliss' death, it's appropriate to think of September as an automobile awareness month, culminating inInternational Car Free Day. September 22nd is the day that cyclists, transit access activists, and municipalities the world over celebrate a moment of independence from the automobile.

But with the local Smart Commute Challenge moving to the spring (it will return in April 2008) and neither Durham nor Chapel Hill hosting any Car Free Day celebrations, September 22nd came and went much like any other day in the Triangle. The Triangle Transit Authority's Fare Free Day, on Friday Sept 21st, was the closest thing going.

Many places around the world celebrate their car free days more enthusiastically. This year, Montreal closed off sections of its historic district to private automobiles on Friday, September 21st. Last spring, Mexico City's Marcelo Ebrard launched a series of weekend efforts to encourage bicycle usage. By closing off selected city streets, the mayor creates ciclovias, or bike paths, on Sundays. Ebrard arguably borrowed the idea from Bogotá, Colombia where approximately 75 miles of its city streets are closed to motor vehicle traffic every Sunday. These car-free programs allow cyclists to gain confidence on the road before relying on their bikes as transportation.

Every day is an automobile awareness day in some parts of London. Since February 2003, London has levied tolls on drivers who take their automobiles into the core of the city. Congestion taxation, as the practice is called, aims to reduce private automobile traffic in dense urban areas by charging drivers fees, then reinvesting the profits in public transportation. Since 2003, congestion in London is down 30%. Michael Bloomberg has openly endorsed a similar tax program for relieving congestion in New York City.

But this September, we took another step backward in the US, another step tpward furthering our dependence on the automobile. A post on Google's official GoogleBlog put out the word that the software giant is soliciting proposals from entrepreneurs who think they can design the next generation of electric hybrid automobiles.

The fact that Google wants a hand in designing electric automobiles is not so surprising,considering that Tesla Motors is a Silicon Valley start-up company. Tesla Motors makes an all-electric Roadster, a $98,000 two-seater that outpaces Ferraris on the drag strip. But perhaps it is because Google is known for outside the box thinking that their request for proposals strikes me as a step in the wrong direction.

Entrepreneurs who answer Google's challenge are likely to produce exactly what it asks for — new designs for electric hybrid automobiles. The continued focus on the automobile is a limitation on creative thinking. A shift from the era of the Ford Mustang and Porsche Cayenne to an era of electric Ford Mustangs and Porsche Cayenne's is not the radical shift in our transportation design that this country needs.

Teslas and Google cars may not run on gasoline (though, as

hybrids the Google cars probably will), and weaning ourselves off petroleum products will surely reduce greenhouse gases. But keeping transit focused on the free-wheeling automobile will do nothing to address the 40,000 deaths per year that result from automobile crashes.

After all, the taxicab that killed Henry Bliss was electric.

*This column appeared in The Herald Sun in October 2007.*

# Cross-country bike trail teaches much about time

She turns around, sees reminders of how far she's ridden, and thinks about how different the world seems when you're on a bike. The hills she's finished climbing look so innocent from a car and feel so challenging on a bike.

She looks ahead and sees how far she has yet to go. The road is arrow straight and flat. Lined with corn and soybean fields on either side, her path stretches to the horizon.

Judy Martell, 55, of Durham is a little less than halfway through riding the American Discovery Trail, a 6,800 mile patchwork of paved greenways, state parks, and roadways connecting Delaware with San Francisco. In 2001, she woke from a dream with a goal to use her own two legs to get her from the Atlantic to the Pacific.

A month ago, she reached St. Louis, Missouri.

If she were to ride the entire Discovery Trail in one effort, she estimates it would take her anywhere from a month to a month and a half. Whether to raise money for a charitable cause, bring attention to an injustice, or just to experience the changing landscape of our vast country on a more human scale, Martell says "there are a lot of people who are doing it straight through on the Discovery Trail, biking or walking."

"I do it in chunks... in sections, because I can't do the logistics of being away from home long enough to do it all in one shot," says Martell. When she knows she's got five free days coming up, she starts to plan the next trip.

For most of the route, she's been riding alone. But friend Alison Carpenter also of Durham recently kept her company from Cincinnati to St. Louis.

Traveling at the speed of a bike allows a different perspective, says Carpenter. "Life's just fleeting from an automobile on a day to day basis. Then you get on a bike... and time just sort of disappears, everything changes, and your perspective becomes 'eat, drink, bike, sleep, bike.' It was definitely a meditative experience."

Carpenter had never done any long-distance bike touring before. "The first day was mentally challenging. We did fifty-five miles in the first day, and I'd never ridden fifty-five miles at once," she says. "[The] second and third were more physically challenging. But, after the third day I felt like, 'alright, I can do this'." By the end of the fifth day she had a hard time letting the trip come to an end.

Her pluck speaks to the *c'est la vie* attitude that got them through parts of their ride; it was not without challenge. Martell lost her GPS device early in the trip. At one point they ended up riding on a limited access freeway with tractor trailers passing a little too close and too fast for comfort. And on their last day, they found themselves riding through the headwinds of a tornado system that hit Illinois later that day.

Nor do they forget the killer leg cramps, a semi-paralyzed left hand, and the ka-chunk of an adjusting chiropractor's table that still rings in their ears.

But, then there was the time they stopped at a restaurant and a pickup truck driver who had passed them thirty miles back welcomed them with a "you made it! Alright, way to go!"

Or the time they rolled up to an auto-auction with a vending machine tucked behind a fence decorated with a "dealers only" sign. After sneaking in to get water from the vending machine one of the dealers struck up a conversation with the two weathered and worn-out cyclists.

And they'll never forget that warm, inviting cafe – with fresh baked bread — in, "where was that cafe again?" Carpenter asks.

Riding through the country side and small towns endeared them to the folks they passed. Martell and Carpenter feel like the people they met along the way would not have been as open or willing to strike up conversations if they'd been just another driver passing through.

Planning for a trip like this is not as difficult as you might think, says Martell. That is, if you plan the way Martell does, it's not that taxing. She likes to leave a lot of the details to just work themselves out. But, not without reason.

"I think we get into this box of 'it's a scary world and let's stay in our safe route'. But when you put yourself out there, then you're reminded that the world's not that scary. Life is going on in these little towns just like it is here. It's just a different pace in a different place," she says.

"A yearning for pure spontaneity is human nature," says Carpenter, "but at the same time that time runs together on [a trip like this], it also becomes more precious."

*This column appeared in The Herald Sun in December 2005.*

# Bike couriers spur alleycats

Remember the childhood fun of a scavenger hunt? You and your friends run around the backyard or school yard, gathering clues in corners or under rocks. Sometimes the clues stared you in the face, but the excitement of the game obscured them from view. And for some of them, there was a goal and even a winner. But that wasn't really the point. The point was to have fun, right?

Take a scavenger hunt, mix in a little punk culture, anti-authoritarian politics, and a taste of danger, spread the course out over town, and make it a bike race. Now, you've got what's called an alleycat.

Although only a handful of people showed up to Durham's St. Patrick's Day alleycat, they came from as far away as Hillsborough, Raleigh, and New Haven, Connecticut. OK, Mark didn't come to Durham just for the race; Yale Divinity School was on spring break and he was in town visiting old friends. But Eric Owens, organizer of the event, isn't surprised that folks came up from Raleigh for the ride.

"It's really growing at an exponential rate right now. Many small towns the size of Durham are now hosting alleycats, whereas a few years ago no one had heard of them," says Owens. So, where did they come from?

Alleycat races are an outgrowth of the bike courier scenes of major metropolitan areas. In cities like Chicago, New York, or San Francisco, the downtown centers are so densely packed that frequently the fastest way to get a letter, memo, filing, or other parcel from one side of town to another is by bicycle. Courier companies employ bikers to navigate through car, bus, and truck-filled streets, and because the courier is paid by delivery, efficiency is key to being a successful messenger.

Efficiency on a bike in a dense urban area, however, often translates into speed, disregard for traffic laws (it might be more convenient to ride the wrong way on a one-way street, for example), and a significant element of risk-taking.

The risks of the job, thinks Owens who spent a year as a bike messenger in Manhattan before coming to Duke for graduate school, bond the couriers together. Bragging about delivering this many packages over that big an area is something he heard regularly after work.

And an alleycat race is the place to settle the bragging rights, to see once and for all who is the fastest or who knows the city the best. "They grow out of a culture of work," says Owens.

An alleycat is a unique sort of race. It's designed to recreate the day-to-day challenges of messengers. At the Durham alleycat, each rider received a manifest made up of checkpoints throughout town. To complete the manifest, each rider had to visit each checkpoint and document somehow that he or she had been there.

For instance, to prove that they'd been to Cookout on Hillsborough Rd, riders had to write down the number of milkshake flavors the restaurant offers. Hand-written signs hung near the top of several parking garages downtown, and racers had to scribble down the signs' messages. And one checkpoint was simply to write down what's at 1825 Chapel Hill Rd. Riders had to go there to find out.

Unlike other cycling races, alleycats are not held on closed courses. They're held in the streets, where riders mix with other traffic. Nor is there a prescribed route; riders complete the manifest in whatever order they want. So in addition to being a test of speed, an alleycat tests how well riders know local landmarks and streets.

But, without a bike messenger scene in the Triangle, why are there alleycats?

"Now that skateboarding culture has been completely co-opt-

115

ed, is mainstream, and you can find everything you need at the mall, I think people are looking for the next underground thing," says Owens. Since alleycats are not sanctioned bike races, they have a certain chic factor to them.

So, did the St. Pat Alleycat bring together an emerging Triangle urban-bike scene? I'm really not sure. But it was fun, a little absurd, and no one got hurt.

*This column appeared in The Herald Sun in April 2006.*

# Doping scandals spoiling the spirit of sports

Allegations that cyclists are doping are so common that anyone accused is guilty until proven innocent. And that's taking its toll on the sport. The cover of the October Bicycling, arguably the sport's leading monthly, makes plain why it matters – whether Floyd Landis doped or didn't, "either way, we lose."

Did Landis pull off one of the greatest accomplishments in

cycling's history? The night before stage 17 of this year's Tour de France, Floyd Landis told his wife he was going to "go out in the morning and do something big." He attacked – broke away from his competitors, setting his own maniacal pace – so early in the day that most thought he had no chance of following through. When you attack like he did you ride on your own, without the wind-breaking assistance of the peloton or even your own team. He went on to win stage 17, setting himself up to win the Tour.

Or, did he pull off an incredible fraud? A few days after being crowned champion of the Tour, a blood sample tested positive for irregularities – an unnaturally high ratio of testosterone to epitestosterone.

There are good reasons to doubt that he cheated. Testosterone is an anabolic steroid: a muscle-builder. It's the choice of weight lifters or sprinters, not endurance athletes. Testosterone helps an athlete only cumulatively. Over time, it helps an athlete amass muscle – more quickly, yes, but it's not an instant effect. If Landis was using synthetic testosterone for a performance boost, traces of it would have shown up prior to stage 17.

Besides, testosterone is produced naturally by the body and the human body is complex in ways that continue to baffle scientists. In addition to controlling muscle-growth, testosterone regulates bone density. A few days into the Tour, Landis announced he was suffering necrosis of the hip and was scheduled for hip surgery immediately following the Tour.

Human performance, at the level of a professional athlete, is a matter of refined efficiency. Do we know that the human body, especially one tuned as efficiently as Landis' and suffering a degenerative bone disease, could not independently and naturally slow its production of epistestosterone and accelerate its production of testosterone as a matter of survival? Landis may be right; he may not be able to give a good explanation of his blood sample.

If he successfully defends himself, Landis may recover his place on a pro-team and maybe even his reputation. He may keep his title to the TdF, but the damage seems to be done. The culture of drug-use in sports is so pervasive (or at least apparently so) that we're ready to believe the accused are guilty before all the evidence is in and without understanding the contested accuracy of the blood testing techniques.

About the only thing going for cycling's continuing dope-scandal plague is that it's not just cycling's problem. The U.S. Congress held special hearings in 2005 to investigate alleged drug use in Major League Baseball and is currently holding similar hearings investigating steroid use in the National Football League. Earlier this summer, Marion Jones and Justin Gatlin, international level track athletes, each failed doping tests andsubsequently lost their multi-million dollar contracts with Nike.

The real problem is that while the margin between winning and losing is usually small on the clock, it's much bigger in the paycheck.

Athletes competing at the elite professional level live or die by the fractions of seconds between finishes. Taking any amount of drugs won't make me ride as fast as Landis, but it might give someone who is already training as hard as Landis the boost he needs to edge out a competitor. And there's his incentive.

The difference in lifestyle between a first place finisher and a fifth place finisher is more exaggerated than the differing times it takes them to cross the finish line. Corporate money in sports is corrupting sport itself. And it's the willingness to be bought, that most capitalist of virtues, that infects the players and brings the gods of physical performance down to our very human level.

Don't believe me? Tell me (and without Googling it) who finished second to Lance in each of his seven Tour de France wins. Or, this year, who stood in the third place spot on the podium while Landis stood on top? We don't know because OLN, Nike, Campagnolo, Phonak, Gerolsteiner, and everyone else who has money in sports reward one spot: the top of the podium.

What's the answer to doping in sports? I don't know... I don't have an answer, but I think a worthy pursuit in life is to ask questions the answers to which cannot be Googled. It's often useful just to articulate the problem, and that may be all we can do.

The growing popularity of single-speed rallies (Happy Fun Racing hosts one locally each year) and alleycats (five in the Triangle area so far in 2006) speaks to the growing uneasiness with the one-winner-one-reward paradigm. Weekend alleycats have traditional race elements, as does the Single Speed World Championship, but their rewards range from tattoos to messenger bags and bike parts, which are often distributed more democratically. They're often more anti-race, and more fun.

The monthly Tuesday night Cruiser Ride – Carrboro's social ride praising the virtues of low-tech and slow pace – is no race at all. It's a creative reminder that riding a bike is supposed to be fun.

*This column appeared in The Herald Sun in September 2006.*

Entrance gate to the velodrome (Buenos Aires, Argentina)

# Some athletes lose sight of sportsmanship of biking

Jan Ulrich and Ivan Basso lost their bids for the yellow jersey to Operation Puerta before this year's Tour de France even began.

Operation Puerta isn't a new contender for victory; it's a six-month doping investigation and arguably the most significant doping scandal of bicycle racing. Thanks to OP, thirteen professional riders were kicked out of the race and more than forty others are involved in a continuing investigation.

Around the same time Operation Puerta's news was breaking, Lance Armstrong was wrapping up his latest victory. He settled a libel suit with a British newspaper that had accused him of using banned drugs to speed his recovery from cancer and boost him to a Tour de France victory in 1999.

What's at issue when cyclists are accused of doping is whether or not professional athletes have cheated. The Tour de France is a stage race, spanning nearly a month with riders covering up to 130 miles per day with brutal climbing stages in the Alps and Pyrenees. Since stage races in cycling are tests of endurance and aerobic strength, cheating methods revolve around ways to increase the rider's aerobic efficiency.

Did Lance use EPO? Did Jan Ulrich freeze his own blood for a transfusion at a later time? What would it matter if they did? More plainly, what's wrong with doping anyway?

The superficial answer is that doping is against the rules. Every professional sport has a governing body that establishes the rules of the sport and the conditions under which athletes may compete. Doping is breaking the rules of the game. In a sense, it's like goaltending in basketball or slide-tackling in soccer.

But goaltending or slide-tackling can happen by accident, whereas doping is intentional. That's why the penalty for doping is more serious than giving the other team a foul shot or a free kick.

Doping is rule-breaking that you try desperately and secretly to get away with. An athlete caught doping will usually have gone to elaborate lengths to hide it.

In other words, doping is cheating.

For a more meaningful answer to the question what's wrong with doping, we have to see sport in a more meaningful context. And to do this, we turn to the arbiters of meaning – philosophers.

In *The Philosophical Athlete*, Heather Reid says that all sports have moments of challenge – "times when an athlete finds him- or herself alone, faced with a particular task and the very real possibilities of success or failure."

It is these moments of challenge that make sport meaningful. Whether or not you can rise to the challenge – whether the challenge is to make the free throw, outrun a defender, or beat the current best time in a bicycle race – is a matter of discipline and skill. Whether you can do so while respecting your opponents is a matter of personal integrity.

An athlete who dopes disrespects him or herself as well as his/her competitors, officials, and fans.

Without opponents there wouldn't be any competitive sports. Using drugs or blood transfusions to gain an advantage over your competitors is to disrespect your competitors by ignoring the rules of game. Without a competitor, there is no opportunity to win. Opponents are necessary to play the game or race the race. So, respect for your competitors is what fairness in sport is based on.

Cheating (or doping) enters the picture when the desire to win

125

the game supplants the desire to be an athlete who is worthy of winning.

Pop culture's values may be different. On reality TV or in a culture of on-demand instant gratification, cheating is more a strategy to get ahead of your competitor than the forbidden alternative. Indeed, in these nihilistic venues getting caught, rather than cheating, is the sign of weakness.

But the concepts of respect and fairness, archaic as they may sound to some, are still what sport is based on. Training is a performance enhancing activity done in earnest. Preparing for a race, there is no substitute (physically or morally) for practice. If sport is a measure of physical discipline, mental toughness, and moral determination, then cheating leaves us unworthy of playing the game (much less winning).

Without Jan Ulrich, David Zabriske, Ivan Basso, Floyd Landis, or George Hincapie racing against him, Lance Armstrong's seven Tour de France victories would be meaningless. They also would have been meaningless if he hadn't developed the muscle-tone or dexterous precision needed to rocket his body and bike across the French countryside.

*This column appeared in The Herald Sun in July 2006.*

# Can mountain bikers be green?

**M**any mountain bikers pick up the sport as another way to spend time in the woods. But not all trails let an environmentally conscious rider enjoy the ride.

Improperly built trails soon develop deep ruts in the ground and can damage sensitive vegetation, especially if those trails are carved through low-lying areas that stay wet. Perhaps worse are the poorly constructed stunt zones where deep holes are dug or wooden structures are built hastily. If built of untreated lumber, these structures quickly rot becoming both neighborhood blight and safety hazards.

Trails like these exist in the Triangle, though they are usually pirated trails with quasi-legal status. If you ride much in the area, you know which ones I'm talking about.

It doesn't have to be this way; mountain biking and environmental protection go hand in hand. Since the so-called Park City Agreement in 1994 with the International Mountain Biking Association (IMBA), the Sierra Club has recognized mountain biking as a positive, worthwhile outdoor activity. Raleigh resident Bill Camp sums it up best – "mountain biking is a good way for families to spend time together participating in a healthy activity together."

Building environmentally sustainable mountain bike trails is not only possible; through organized education efforts, it's quickly become preferable. Car-manufacturer Subaru and IMBA co-sponsor two Trail Care Crew teams who annually travel the country preaching the gospel of sustainable trails. Their Trailbuilding Schools have taught more than 150,000 people how to build trails right the first time so that they'll last forever.

Jill Van Winkle and Chris Bernhardt, IMBA's east coast Trail Care Crew visited the Triangle in March 2005. The class was packed with volunteers, land managers, and park officials all hungry to learn how to build trails that will withstand the impact of the growing sport. At the end of the weekend, Bernhardt said he was impressed by the local commitment to sustainable trail-building, specifically Durham's Little River Regional Park's singletrack.

Well-built trails draw people to them. The more fat tires turn out on trails, more people will be there to protect wooded areas from development. Unsustainable development, here in the Southeast, is the single largest earth-scarring activity. Our fetish for new strip-malls anchored by big-box retail chains has meant the demise of many favorite homegrown trail systems.

The leadership of the Triangle Off Road Cyclists (TORC) is keenly aware that sprawl threatens access to local trials. "That's one of the reasons TORC was formed," says Camp, who is president of the advocacy group. Through fun events like last month's Fat Tire Festival, Camp hopes to "raise awareness of our trails advocacy and volunteer efforts to build and maintain legal singletrack in the Triangle area."

TORC has its work cut out. Right now, sights are set on new trails – conceived through memoranda of understanding with the landowners and built by volunteers – from northern Wake County down to Chatham County. Thanks to TORC's lobbying efforts, developers' masterplans already include singletrack options at the city of Raleigh's new Forest Ridge park as well as the new park to be developed after the North Wake Landfill closes.

The Briar Chapel subdivision in northern Chatham County is a model for developer/volunteer collaboration. By the time the first houses in the new subdivision go up for sale, the publicly accessible singletrack TORC is building also should be open for business.

In local and regional media outlets, TORC has received flattering media attention for its efforts to preserve established trail systems and grow new ones in a region of North Carolina where sprawl is the norm.

And mountain bikers are generally good stewards of the land. I know of no other sport (organized or otherwise) where the participants take on lobbying for, building, and maintaining their own recreational outlets with the same fervor and tenacity as mountain bikers. Since its inception in 1988, IMBA's members have registered more than 1 million volunteer hours of trail work. Heck, every land manager I've ever met says that mountain bikers out-do all other volunteers when it comes to time spent with a McLeod rake or Pulaski in hand.

Park officials at Beaverdam State Park, Lake Crabtree County Park, and Harris Lake county Park say that on occasion mountain bikers have broken the rules and ridden closed trails but that it hasn't become a problem. Cyclists respect the trails, says Drew Cade, Park Manager at Lake Crabtree.

Even when a vocal minority of environmentalists try to claim that mountain bikers are harmful to the trails, science is on the side of the cyclists. IMBA has gathered on its website an impressive array of independent scientific studies of the environmental effects of mountain biking, all of which reach the conclusion that mountain biking makes no more of an impact on the natural environment than hiking, horseback riding, or other recreational trail activities.

With the right priorities, including a TORC membership card

in your pocket, you can ride local trails knowing that you're doing it in the greenest way.

Now, if only we could grow our greenway and bike-lane infrastructure at the same pace, we could ride to trail-head and leave the car behind. But that's another story.

*This column appeared in The Herald Sun in July 2006.*

Mark Smith rides the teeter-totter at Lake Crabtree County Park (Raleigh, NC)

# Olympics may inspire desire to try mountain biking

The 2004 summer Olympics in Athens have already seen some exciting race results in cycling.

After leaving the Tour de France because of a back injury, Tyler Hamilton won the United States its first-ever gold medal in men's road time trial.

Axel Merckx, son of the legendary five-time Tour winner Eddie Merckx, earned a bronze medal in the men's road race.

Anna Meares and the Australian pursuit team have each broken world records in the velodrome and they aren't even finished racing yet. And all this has happened on skinny tires … the fat tires begin racing tomorrow!

This is only the third Olympics for mountain biking, which debuted in Atlanta's 1996 Olympic Games. Since then, the world of professional mountain biking has reached its halcyon days. The competition will be fierce Friday and Saturday as riders hurl themselves and their bikes down rocky slopes, clearing boulders and dirt jumps alike, approaching 65 mph. Don't miss it!

Pisgah National Forest and the Tsali trail network in the western end of our state draw mountain bikers from all over the country, but you don't need to drive out to there to get in some time off-road. Mountain biking is well-established in the Triangle.

Lake Crabtree County Park has a great network of trails for beginners. Call the park office at 460-3390 to make sure the trails are open when you plan to ride.

New Light is a collection of trails on Wildlife Resources land near Falls Lake. Route 66, one of the trails at New Light, is a favorite, showing off some of the best of what mountain biking is all about.

You can find descriptions of trails and directions to these and many others in the Triangle area atwww.trianglemtb.com. The Durham Orange Mountain Bike Organization (DOMBO, www.dombo-nc.org) is working tirelessly to finish Durham's first mountain biking course. When completed, it will be at the Little River Park off Guess Road in northern Durham County.

To ride the kind of course like in the Olympics, dedicated XC race courses, you can head to the mountains. Ski slopes often open their chairlifts to downhill and cross-country bikers in the summertime.

*This column appeared in The Herald Sun in August 2004.*

Superman watches as Andrew Farris flies, Lake Crabtree County Park (Raleigh, NC)

# Outings introduce kids to dirty fun

This July, my nephew visited from Canada. Matt, 15, is a skilled athlete – a hockey star, a track phenom, a confident snowboarder – and like most teenagers, difficult to impress. As often as he's heard me talk about mountain biking, though, I realized this summer that he'd never ridden singletrack.

I took him for a spin around the trails at Lake Crabtree County Park, and by the fifth mile he was hooked. I could see it in his face. He confessed later on that he'd never experienced anything like it before. I was excited to introduce something meaningful to his life.

Mountain biking can teach riders young and old an appreciation of the natural environment, responsibility for the trails, and a lifetime of active, healthy habits.

These are just a few of the reasons why Congress, for the second year in a row, has designated the first Saturday in October "Take a Kid Mountain Biking Day."

North Carolina and Colorado senators and representatives co-sponsored a joint resolution (SR 195) to support the International Mountain Bike Association's youth-oriented outreach effort.

At 10AM, Saturday October 1st, the Triangle Off-Road Cyclists (TORC) are sponsoring events at three local favorite trail systems.

Volunteers will be on-site at Lake Crabtree County Park in Raleigh, Legend Park in Clayton, and Little River Regional Park in Durham.

Get there early for a skills-building session, where experienced mountain bikers reveal the secret techniques of log-crossing, bunny-hopping, and hill-climbing. Once you've got your skill-set built up, ride leaders will be available to show you the way through the woods.

In their petition to Congress, IMBA cites heightened levels of childhood obesity as one of its reasons for reaching out to kids. In a July press-release, IMBA states its belief that mountain biking builds self-confidence and offers kids and adults "an adrenaline-packed adventure while giving them an effective workout."

IMBA reports that in 2004, thousands of kids participated in more than 100 events nationwide and in several other countries. The international organization expects even greater numbers of participants this year.

At the TORC events, kids age 14 and under need to be accompanied by an adult, and the parks require all riders to wear helmets.

If you need to come up with a set of wheels for the weekend, the Bicycle Chain's Durham and Chapel Hill stores rent mountain bikes for $25-35 a day. The stores also allow you to use up to $50 of rentals as credit toward the purchase of a bike.

Aside from a bike and helmet, bring lots of water and an adventurous spirit.

So c'mon out and bring a kid with you for some good, clean fun in the dirt. Whether you're in elementary school or just a kid at heart, "Take a Kid Mountain Biking Day" will be a fun, active outdoor event.

*This column appeared in The Herald Sun in September 2005.*

Misty morning spotlight, W. Main Street (Durham, NC)

# Solstice night ride brings together diverse group

**B**ack in the winter, Curt and Judy Eshelman had an idea. They though it would be fun to celebrate the summer solstice with an organized cycling event. At night. A night ride in honor of the longest day of the year.

"They made one fatal error," says friend and fellow cyclist Peter Anlyan. "They put it out to the cycling community for opinions."

Phillip Barron

It seems no one could agree on anything – the time, the route, whether to make it a benefit ride. But Curt Eshelman is quick to point out that the idea died for lack of consensus, not a lack of interest.

A week before the solstice, Anlyan and the Eschelmans revived the idea, passed the word among friends, and gathered twenty or more riders at the American Tobacco Campus for a 17 mile ride.

As we head off around 8:30pm, the sun is setting and the riders are giddy. Not many have ever ridden their bikes at night before, and for a good number of the riders, this event is their first foray into group bike rides. Fitting that an ad-hoc event brings together such an unlikely group of people.

"Well, [it's my] first intentional night ride," says Muriel Moody. There was that time, in the Peace Corps, in Madagascar, "but that's a long story." Moody, a first year Duke Law School student getting a jump on her studies this summer, is excited to get tapped into the local cycling community.

For Tate Little, the solstice ride is also his first group ride in Durham. Little moved to Durham only two days before the summer solstice when his girlfriend, Roxanne Hall of Durham's Habitat for Humanity, told him about the ride. Little and Hall are training for the local MS 150 ride in September. "I'd just like to get in as many rides as I can," says Little. "This is a nice, safe ride."

Hall says she can't believe all the fireflies. It's "nice and cool. I'm really enjoying it. It's a different experience. Durham by night."

Rusty Miller, a cycling coach and "ex-professional cyclist" joins the ride midway through it. On his way home from his own ride, he spots a pack of riders with lights. "A night time ride on the Tobacco Trail... how could I say 'no'?"

Near the end of our route, we cross the bridge over Lakewood Avenue. Any hint of sunlight is gone; the sky is a deep blue-gray. Facing north, all you can see are the lights of Durham's skyline and the blinking tail-lights of other cyclists.

As rider Matt DeMargel puts it, the solstice was the "perfect night for it."

*This column appeared in The Herald Sun in July 2005.*

Another misty morning (Research Triangle Park, NC)

# Falling just a beneficial part of bicycling

All cyclists have stories about accidents: the first time, the worst time, the most recent time. Falling, in my opinion, is just part of cycling. For the most part, especially if you're wearing your helmet, falling isn't so bad. It gives you the chance to get back up.

On the way to work a few months ago, a familiar corner of the last 50 yards of my commute revealed itself as unfamiliar. Rounding the corner, I tried to keep as much speed as possible for the climb up the steep hill on the other side. The corner, a sharp right turn, is the only thing standing between me and the momentum I need to coast up at least a quarter of the hill. My 9-mile commute is not hard, but by the time I get to this hill, my feet are heavy.

Seeing how fast I can take the corner is one of the risks I take to challenge myself on my way to work. Every morning I go a little faster, lean the bike a little more, and make myself a little more vulnerable. But, this morning, I rode a little too fast or leaned a little too far. It was tropical storm season, and the suddenly clear blue sky belied the fact that it had rained persistently for three days. Although the roads were dry, under the canopy of the trees the trail was still wet.

Wet pavement, hit at an angle and with enough speed, can be slick as ice. It doesn't take much mud, wet grass, or algae slime to pull a wheel out from under you. Especially if you're braking into the turn. I should have finished braking before the turn, so that I could accelerate through it. But, my confidence was off and I was still braking while turning. Probably because I was afraid of falling.

The front tire slipped first. The bottom of the front wheel kicked out and to the left. The rest of the bike, not prepared to follow the front wheel's new direction and keep a 200-pound rider on top, laid down on its right side. By the time the rear wheel was sliding, the handlebars hit the path, bounced, and skidded down the hill. The bike came to a stop about 15 feet away from where the front tire slipped. With a smoothly worn bar-end, the bike faired better than I.

I slid across the pavement on it. The sliding didn't hurt, even though skin was tearing. It hurt only afterward. While you're falling and sliding on pavement, it's almost like it's not happening to you. You don't have time to think or feel.

When I stood up, I began to feel. Yeah, my shoulder hurt from the jarring impact, but it didn't dislocate. Yeah, my hip hurt from slamming into pavement, but I had no trouble walking. Yeah, I was bleeding from my elbow, but not badly considering what just happened.

What I felt most was relief. Relief that I was OK; that my fears didn't come true. Later, I was even glad that I had fallen. I felt like I had accomplished something important.

As we age, we grow more fragile. We lose the adept strength, flexibility, and elasticity of our childhood physiques. But our habits accelerate the biological inevitability of aging. We are less active as adults than we are as children. We value play less; we value physical activity less. We surround ourselves with safety features like airbags, surge protectors, carbon monoxide detectors and surveillance cameras. For many of us if we play, we tend to play it safe.

This is something to think about. We're not just growing more fragile as we grow older, we're also growing more conservative. Some of us take fewer risks because we see risk as a health care liability or a threat to job security.

What are we afraid of? Maybe we're afraid of falling because we don't fall often enough. We fear falling when we forget that falling is about healing, about recovering, about learning.

Phillip Barron

If we fell more, we'd be a little bruised, maybe a little bloody, a little more sore. But, we'd be better prepared for what comes next. Where we fall and bounce back, where we risk and succeed, where we work through fear, that's where we find meaning in life.

*This column appeared in The Herald Sun in January 2005.*

# About the Author

Devoted to the humanities, Phillip Barron is a writer and award-winning digital media artist living in Davis, California. His writings appear in academic journals as well as magazines and newspapers. Barron has taught philosophy at the Chapel Hill and Greensboro campuses of the University of North Carolina, developed digital media projects at the National Humanities Center, and now works in digital history at the University of California, Davis.

# Durham Resources

BPAC: Durham Bicycle and Advisory Commission
http://www.bikewalkdurham.org/

Durham Bike and Ped listserve
http://groups.yahoo.com/group/durhambikeandped/

Durham Bike Co-op
http://www.durhambikecoop.org/

Carolina Tarwheels Bicycle Club
http://www.tarwheels.org/

Halloween Hundred and Bull Moon Ride
http://www.durhamhabitat.org/

TORC: Triangle Off-Road Cyclists
http://www.torc-nc.org/

Triangle MTB message board
http://www.trianglemtb.com/

CPSIA information can be obtained at www.ICGtesting.com
Printed in the USA
BVOW050358121011

273435BV00005B/2/P